Do You Get It?

Understanding Racism in the Workplace

BARBARA MCDONALD

DEDICATION

For my beloved parents and all the inspirational figures
fighting for the fair and equal treatment of all people in
the world.

TABLE OF CONTENTS

*

ACKNOWLEDGMENTS

My gratitude to the Divine. At no time in my life did I ever entertain the idea of writing a book. It just goes to show that you never can tell.

To all those precious gems who blessed my life from childhood but are no longer with us. Thank you for your friendships, your protection, your guidance, and your love.

To my soul sisters who have stood by my side always. I love you all to the heavens and beyond, always.

To Stephen Taylor, thank you for your valuable feedback on an earlier draft of this book in 2022, it was most appreciated.

Forward

It has been 30 years since the loss of a beautiful young soul on UK shores. The loss was because he had a different skin colour. His life challenges and his aspirations did not matter to those who took his life, or to those entrusted to achieve justice for the loss, because he had a different skin colour. The pain of his family's loss was my pain and the pain of all dark skin people because we have a different skin colour.

Dark skin people did not stand alone in feeling this injustice, people of all skin colours stood up against the travesty. The lost life of Stephen Lawrence would not be just another murder victim to racism, but an influence for change. Our loss became rooted within equality legislation and saw the creation of the equality duty. This tree of new life achieved a new chapter in the race relations movement in the UK that went beyond the differences of skin colour. It influenced changes in social attitudes towards differences found in all people, whether in relation to their race, age, gender, ability, religion, sexuality, belief, or marital status.

Strengthening the UK equality law promoted diversity and recognition of the benefits that a multicultural society can achieve socially and economically. Many organisations promoted a diverse workforce and valued the talents that difference achieved whether through increased profit margins, diverse product reach or improved service provision. All skin colours were engaged in this equality drive because we all believed in its benefits. Strategies were formulated to remove inequality and to ensure that difference in all its forms were no longer the recipients of less favourable treatment.

Yet not everyone believed nor cared to transform. The preference to retain racist traditions is the cause of the explosion of 'disproportionate' and 'culturally toxic' themed reports seen on current media platforms. The great work and commitment of those champions to embed equal treatment in the workplace, from the specialists, human resources practitioners, managers, and employees, seems to have been in vain with inclusion becoming nothing more than an illusion.

Let us be clear, disproportionate treatment means less favourable treatment, which is unlawful discrimination. How then can this problem be turned around without there being another life lost to racism or sexism or any other protected characteristic? There is no one definitive answer but the enforcement of a zero-tolerance culture and building an awareness of less favourable treatment in the workplace, is a starting point.

The purpose of this book aims to smash through the illusions of inclusion and to expose inequality within the workplace, from a different perspective. From my perspective. This insight into the business activities inhibiting a truly inclusive workplace will hopefully equalise the workplace level playing field for all employees with a protected characteristic.

There is no intention to demonise white privilege because in truth, it serves no purpose and quite frankly it is refreshing that its existence is finally universally acknowledged. There will, however, be the flipping the privilege workplace coin to provide insight into those business systems, processes and practices that refuse to allow difference to step into the privilege domain.

It made sense to speak of my own experience as a dark skin socially labelled black female, who has experienced racism in the workplace. I do not however, disclose my personal experiences lightly and only do so because I need for you to get it and to understand workplace equality from a different perspective. What organisations, may view as beneficial to employees with a protected characteristic, may be a cause of detriment. The mutually agreed terms of the employment contract offered to all employees, are often weaponised by delegated powerholders ~~on an ego trip,~~ to abuse, manipulate, or sabotage the careers of dark skin employees. Whether knowingly or not, such conduct crosses the line from an expected level of professionalism into racism, where ignorance is not an accepted legal justification.

Whilst I aim to concentrate on employment matters, there is some digression into my personal life as there appears to be a need for some to gain a better understanding of the social disadvantages experienced by dark skin employees. There is plenty of information on the various media platforms to enlighten those seeking this knowledge. That said, it is hoped that my disclosure will remove the burden placed on those unsuspecting dark skin employees who, if they share my view, merely wish to be recipients of the same level of respect and benefits afforded to other employees, rather than be seen as a token gesture.

My working life has been spent predominantly in public sector organisations although my early years were within commercial sectors, and neither experience were void of discriminatory conduct. Having financed most of my further educational studies in Business and Finance, and Human Resource Management, my career path has varied from being an employee with line responsibilities, to managing a team and resources before finally contracting as a human resources practitioner. This pathway now concludes with the imparting of my experiences to encourage organisational members, whether senior leaders, managers, or employees, to better understand and eliminate workplace racism.

The changing nature of work with modern technology and the shifting priorities of individual values following the 2020 covid pandemic, now poses a threat to the survival of organisations that conserve outdated traditions towards difference. The disproportionate treatment of employees will have no doubt contributed towards the generation X workforce exodos. With newer and easier means of achieving independent incomes, one can only wonder how these organisations will continue to survive where the illusion of inclusion is no more. As my parents use to say,

'If you can't hear, you must feel'.

INTRODUCTION

Let me tell you a little about my personal journey into why I wrote this book.

I know racism and it knows me.

It is a part of my life which I live with, and it walks alongside me, day after day after frigging day, that it is exhausting.

Racism is the ice-cold boulder that has shackled itself to me unjustly since childhood.

It does not care that I have a heart, that I have a brain, that I have feelings, that I have ambitions, that I too have a dream, and that I too am human.

Racism only wants to suppress me, in poverty, in mind-set, in living, in being, in life.

Just so that it can be something that it is not and will never be. Like me.

On calling a loved one to wish them a happy sixth birthday, I entered the excited chatter of innocence and inquisitiveness with a child whose beautiful soul shone brightly. It was only after finishing the conversation that I realised tears were steaming down my face.

The conversation had taken me to a place of being a six-year-old running around full of the joys of life, being inquisitive, being comical, being naughty, being a child. I remember the age fondly and being surrounded by the people I love, the soul tribe of my parents, my sisters and extended family members. I remember the lack too, of not having enough of anything, of mom working where she could whilst dad worked night shifts, but we had each other. As sisters we did everything together, one of my sisters who is the funniest person I know was constantly by my side that people mistook us for twins.

Being six years old was a poignant time of my life, because I had an innocent passion for life before it was extinguished. My mom suffered a nervous breakdown resulting in my sisters and I being taken away from our safe haven by white skin social workers, to a cold soulless place of a children's home ran by white skin nuns. So public institutions and controlling mechanisms introduced and latched itself onto me at the tender age of six, where my education was spent in Roman Catholic schools until the age of sixteen.

For the most part we, my sisters and I, were surrounded by white skin people and racism was a daily occurrence whether from other kids, adults, or nuns, it followed us daily. The occasional fist fight to assert myself was a necessary development process when growing up, even though I hated fighting. I was labelled a *'hard knock'* after one fight in secondary school that I was baited by any new hopefuls who wanted the title for themselves. I always did my best not to engage because with age you begin to know better and nothing original had been added to Collins or Oxford dictionaries.

Someone did try their luck and had spent most of the school day walking or siting behind me, provoking and calling me all the racist names they could think of, which was not many. Then on last break in the lower school playground, I sat quietly reading a women's magazine (for educational purposes of course! It could have been a Woman's Own magazine because any Mills & Boon book took too frigging long to get to the point!!). Then my racist friend appeared with their wimpy sidekick coaxing them to fight me, but I wasn't biting. I simply moved to another bench to park myself and reconnect to the ~~juicy~~ educational literature that I was reading. Then she said something that no person should ever say to another, and I lost all self-control.

The feedback from the boys from my English language class who were finishing off an art project on the third floor of

8

the school building, was that I held the girl by their hair and punched her as if I was Mohammed Ali. The two female teachers monitoring in the girl's playground tried but failed to break us apart, and so it took two male teachers jumping out of the staff room window on the ground floor, to pull me off the girl, allegedly. We became friends whilst waiting to be punished outside the headmistress' office where she apologised and explained the reason for her behaviour. This pleased the Headmistress who still gave us a week's detention which had to be spent writing lines from any ~~erotic~~ educational book that we were currently reading.

The point is that I learnt the lesson early about racism where if proven unsuccessful in its direct form, it would find another way in its pursuit to cause maximum harm. Overt racism of name calling in the playground adapted into a covert form to suppress and to deter a person from having anything beyond what they were given. Being the butt of a teacher's jokes, or being continually ignored even when you are the only pupil in the class with your hand in the air to answer a question, became some of the new methods. Discussing future goals with career advisers and being told you could not do something that you have a passion for because *'It's not the done thing'* or *'It's not*

9

what you people do ' or *'Have you thought of becoming a nurse?'* were the stereotypical statements that made me more resilient, more determined to have the life that I wanted and not one that I was *'allowed'* to live. The child in me could not understand this difference in treatment, and the youth in me wanted to prove people wrong but this initial determination transformed me as a young adult into proving to myself that I can, that I am able and that I am possible.

By the time I left secondary school, there were more diverse ethnicities in the community and so too at my school. I had also established a great group of close friends, who were my other soul tribe as we had much in common. We were diverse in ethnicities yet saw no skin colour. They were my protectors and I theirs. My brothers and sister from other mothers were:

Anthony H - I am so proud of all your achievements. You did exactly what you said you would.

Anthony C - I hope you found all the happiness in life that you were searching for.

Wasi M - I hope you realised that you were always worthy and a great success.

Rosemary N - I hope that you are healing the world as you planned.

Maurice M - The smartest man I knew and a billionaire in the making, I hope you made it.

Abdullah Y - I hope you found your kingdom, young Prince.

When I was a youth, racism was overt, but as an adult it had transformed so as not to be detected by the law. The challenge was to identify those acts that continued to disadvantage people like me. In its covert form, you instinctively felt its aura but then it would quickly shapeshift into another guise. But I see where you hide and the types of childish games that you like to play. It's time to expose you because I have had enough of your bullshit. I am done with you, and you will be done with, soon.

PART ONE

'If You Can't Hear…'.

'If you can't hear, you must feel' were the famous words my Jamaican parents would tell me and my sisters when growing up. These words were usually followed by a hot strap, or slipper, or whatever they could lay their hands on to whip our behinds whenever we failed to do as we were told. It signalled a warning to listen or face the consequences of your actions.

The worst punishments were those slaps that occurred in between each syllable of a word uttered, which meant that you hoped for a short sentence. Lord help you if you ever answered back because if you did, you knew that your butt would be sore for weeks.

'*Me*'…whack!...*'tell'*….whack!....*'you*'…whack!….*'fe*'… whack!..*'go*'…whack!…*'buy*'…whack!...*'a*'..whack!…*'bockle*'. .whack!..*'a*'…whack!…*'milk*'….whack!….*'an*'…whack!...*'no*' …whack!…*'fe*'….whack!….*'spen*'….whack!.....*'out*'...whack! …*'di*' …whack! …*'change*'….whack!

My parents are no longer with us in the physical, but their words continue to guide our blossoming family tree and channel through me and my sisters onto those younger members of our soul tribe. The words serve as a warning to do the right thing and to listen to sound advice because if you ignore or act contrary to the advice given, then karma will play its hand.

So, I am sharing these precious words with you. As with my work life experiences, these are disclosed to show that we have more in common than our differences.

CHAPTER ONE

Social Inequality

There is a preference not to discuss colonialism because this stain on humanity is honestly nothing to be proud of. I do not blame those living today for the murderous and inhumane acts that were founded upon the greed of forefathers. However, I do attribute blame towards those people who use their platforms to project and perpetuate racist beliefs, attitudes, and behaviours designed to conserve an outdated and toxic ways of existing.

When reflecting upon my negative life experiences of having a different skin colour to the host population, it was difficult not to make generalised comparisons of the unfair treatment received in these modern times with the days of old. For example:

• Instead of shackles, dark skin people are bound and trapped in social systems where the minimum is provided by controlling political structures.

• Instead of the denial of an education, the learning provided by educational establishments focus on the host population's perceived achievement whilst disregarding the contributions of other ethnicities.

14

- Law enforcement protection rights remains a privilege for the host population while dark skin people receive disproportionate treatment, because of they are perceived as having no rights.

- Instead of the selling of slaves, dark skin people are seen as commodities to be utilised to build the wealth of economies at minimum cost, and to be dispensed with at will.

- Instead of being whipped, castrated, raped or lynched when seeking fairness and freedom, the voices of dark skin people are simply silenced, smothered by the priorities given to any other subject matter.

Many equality and diversity books will inform its readers of there being distinct differences in the treatment of enslaved Africans in the USA when compared to those enslaved by Europeans. The difference from my own perspective is merely one of location. When one considers the amount of slave code literature produced at the time which guided owners on how to produce the 'ideal slave', guidance which was universally applied, one can only reach the same conclusion. Any difference in the treatment of slaves would have depended upon whether a slave worked in the field or in the slave owner's house. My guess is that the difference rested upon the method of abuse endured.

Public Inequality

The rights for equal treatment, to dignity and to life, have been one enduring and exhausting battle for dark skin people to fight. The societal drive for change saw the USA and UK mirror each other by delivering policies that encouraged inclusion but tended to favour the host population whilst covertly perpetuating racism. Take for example the treatment of dark skin soldiers during the world wars. In the book '*White Privilege*' by Susan Rosenberg, the chapter by Karen Brodkin titled '*How the Jews became White Folks*' details the difference in treatment towards dark skin GIs when compared to white skin GIs. The unfair treatment towards those who served their countries is not dissimilar to the UK's treatment of dark skin soldiers from its colonies. Unremembered - Britain's Forgotten War Heroes | All 4 (channel4.com)

The mistreatment continued with the rebuilding of the UK economy with the Government's call for help to the colonies saw dark skin people bring their skills to the UK. Their reward was to be pigeonholed into low paying roles that the host population refused to carry out. My parents' arrival into the UK from the Caribbean was around a decade or so after 'Windrush' and they too endured unfair accommodation, employment and other social challenges when attempting to survive within the country viewed as the motherland. I can only imagine that the challenges they endured would have been not so dissimilar to what people face today in the current cost-of-living crisis but without any means of financial support from the government. Having to rely on the goodwill of friends and relatives who were going through the same challenges, in addition to enduring everyday overt racism, one cannot help but admire their resilience.

Yet if we jump ahead to recent times, the Windrush generation and their families became the target of the current government's strategy aimed to send them back home. The destruction of dark skin people's lives was met with feeble apologies and avoidance strategies rather than constructive effort to resolve this miscarriage of treatment in a timely manner. Windrush generation: Who are they and why are they facing problems? - BBC News

There are too many instances of inequality in everyday situations, far too many. Those responsible for governing our countries around the world are accountable and responsible for protecting and maintaining the wellbeing of all its citizens so that they may live their best lives. Working hard and paying

17

taxes which contribute to the funding of the public services affords us all with such rights in the UK. Yet these public services appear to deny a quality service to those citizens whose skin colour differs from the host population. The evidence of this hostility is not restricted to one bill or strategy but is systemic through the culture, the policies, and the delivery of the public services. The increasing public reports about the '*disproportionate*' treatment towards dark skin people in the UK is somewhat alarming. Take for example, those reports on the National Health Services (NHS) which include:

• Ethnic Health Inequalities in later Life: The Persistence of Disadvantage from 1993 – 2017 published Nov 2021 by Universities of Sussex and Manchester Ethnic health inequalities in later life | Centre for Ageing Better (ageing-better.org.uk)

• NHS risks losing one third of ethnic minority doctors due to racism by the British Medical Authority (BMA) published June 2022 NHS risks losing one third of ethnic minority doctors due to racism, finds BMA report - BMA media centre - BMA

• Race discrimination of oversea specialists whom the NHS rely on to support its service. Reports commissioned by the NHS Race & Health Observatory; reports conducted by the

18

British Medical Association, to name but a few. Race inequalities and ethnic disparities in healthcare - Race equality in medicine - BMA

• The Covid-19 pandemic exposure of the unprecedented number of dark skin people who died in the UK, is pending. Although in March 2023, there are claims that this report will be whitewashed to disregard the impact on ethnic groups.

Any constructive recommendations offered to resolve these '*disproportionate*' treatments are often met with empty gestures by ministers that serve as a poor attempt to appease public discord rather than implementing meaningful solutions to address the problems. The lack of constructive measures to remove inequality embedded within these services, through its culture and leadership, policies, and practices, means that systemic racism prevails. This is why inequality continues to be an everyday challenge for dark skin people. Government inaction can only be viewed as an advocation for the less favourable treatment.

Migration is not a modern concept as people have travelled from one part of the world to settle in another over the centuries. Yet today's migrants entering the UK through unsafe routes are not recognised as vulnerable or as having a protected

19

characteristic. Much has been reported on the ill-conceived and unjust Nationality Boarders bill in the media but learning that the bill provides for a lone travelling young person to be *'scientifically assessed'* in place of the attempt to locate relatives to verify their age, is shocking. The option to force boats crossing the British Channel back into European waters thereby denying migrants any rights, even possibly to life itself left me lost for words and wondering how could a person not compare this modern-day treatment to the slave code? The controversial one-way travel ticket for refugees to an offshore detention centre for *'processing'*, whether in Rwanda or any other country, is comparable to cattle ranching and slave trading. The reports from organisations such as the British Broadcasting Corporation (BBC), Amnesty International, the Law Society, to name a few has helped to bring this travesty to the public's attention. It begs the question of who is the lesser of the two evils, the people traffickers who have yet to be targeted for their crimes, or the UK government for its policy.

In contrast, people fleeing the war in Ukraine travelling to the UK using established safe routes set up by the UK government are treated differently and are provided with access to the same social benefits as UK citizens. It appears that favourable treatment is determined by whether 'safe routes' are utilised. Given that there are no established safe routes for those refugees who resort to using traffickers to flee wars or persecution in other parts of the world, skin colour seems to be the most obvious reason for the less favourable treatment.

Such unfair treatment towards migrants was highlighted in the government's equality impact assessment on this policy prior to its implementation, which was disregarded. So not only are people subjected to both direct and indirect discrimination because of their race and any other protected characteristics, but they are all unfairly categorised as a national security risk. Nationality and Borders Bill: equality impact assessment - GOV.UK (www.gov.uk)

When the government's Rwanda plan was set in motion, appeals to the high court by objectors was turned down by a presiding judge that it took the European Courts of Human Rights to intervene and overturn the UK ruling. This speaks volumes about the discernment of those decision makers, who use their platforms to manipulate established laws for their biased agendas whilst disregarding the established protection of the rights of all humans. Logic would have dictated the creation of a bill that targeted the people traffickers and the establishment

21

of safe travel routes thereby mitigating or eliminating the influx of refugees on British coastal towns. As it currently stands, this bill is not fit for purpose.

Education

This National bill made me question the education standards of its creators, leaders, and decision makers and whether the subjects of morals, ethics or values had been omitted from their educational curriculum. It also made me wonder whether the lecturers of these individuals were presently hanging their heads in shame, given that many of those governing our country have proven themselves to be inept leaders. Categorical imperative, indeed.

The quality of our education influences our character, our skills and our passions, it shapes the people that we will become in life. Education that incorporates the factual historical events of diverse people and cultures in Britain would go some way to building inclusivity and remove the fear of difference. Yet this seems to be a challenge within educational establishments.

A young dark skin recruitment consultant regaled to me his education experience of learning about colonialism and imperialism in his secondary school. Regrettably, the quality of the teaching only served to reinforce the notion of dark skin people inferiority in the world. As a result of this, he spent much of his time fighting to defend himself from classmates who saw him as a lesser human being.

Conversely, my education a few decades earlier centred on white Britishness with no reference to black contributions and influences in the world at all. My real education and learning of my own heritage, aside from watching Arthur Hailey's *'Roots'*, began after leaving school and speaking with my parents. Then through my work with the Handsworth Employment Scheme's Afro-Caribbean Cultural and Educational Agency, where alongside a group of people we promoted Caribbean culture in primary and secondary schools. The slave trade did not feature in any of these sessions, only stories about influential people and the different lifestyles of children around the world, which always ended with the favourite fables of Anancy and his crafty antics.

Given that the UK is a multicultural society, it is surprising that cultural studies is not an essential and mandatory requirement in schools to aid in the objective of a socially inclusive environment. Young minds can only benefit from such education because as adults, they will engage more with other ethnicities from around the world.

Reflecting upon my miseducation, I am reminded of my father when as a young child I went crying to him saying that a nun had called me a black monkey. His response was to laugh and say, '*Ah what, she neva hear of white monkey?*' It was the most profound statement that remains with me to this day. There is no one way of looking at and understanding the things that you are told. Educating oneself is now more accessible beyond traditional methods which enable people to interrogate rather than accept one soul source of information. If I were accepting of all I was taught in the classrooms, I would believe that morals and ethics which belie the foundations of our western society were founded on the thoughts of Greek philosophers and not those from whom they obtained their education and knowledge, from dark skin people.

Do you get it? Inclusion begins with education at any age without reinforcing archaic attitudes or misinformation. Black history consigned to cultural studies in everyday teaching rather than to a month each year would be a significant step in the right direction.

CHAPTER 2

The Corporate Equality Agenda

When we think of all the countless organisations that operate around the world, we do not automatically think of them as exploiting the people whom they employ to provide a service or to create a product. Yet on closer inspection there exists informal structures within these organisations that suppresses the talents and pay of employees. The glass ceiling is typically seen as a barrier restricting women from achieving status at the high table of organisations. Imagine then, the glass ceiling existing at every level within the structure that a dark skin employee must shatter if progression is to be earned.

Organisations who promote inclusivity through a variety of policies and strategies, whether special awareness events or mentoring schemes, are actively engaging with stakeholders who have a protected characteristic. These strategies aim to build trust within internal and external relationships and one such event that takes place yearly in October is Black History month. Whilst some organisations use the month to promote their commitment to diversity, others, unfortunately, use the event only to target the black pound.

25

Following the horrific and public murder of George Floyd in 2020 and the subsequent global uproar that followed, organisations made attempts to demonstrate their anti-racist commitment in a variety of ways. Television advertisements in the UK for example, changed dramatically. Prior to the incident, the products and services advertised by companies very rarely featured dark skin actors, which made one question whether they were living in a multi-cultural society. Then the sudden explosion of dark skin actors on our screens made a friend liken the saturation to black exploitation. This noticeable change however, led me to wonder whether these organisations were taking advantage of the public outcry with token gestures and meaningless lip service, or were they truly committed to inclusion.

Images of Inclusion

The previous chapter provided an example on how racial difference is used as a political tool of exclusion. Commercial organisations on the other hand, have utilised the diverse cultures in society for business advantages. It is not surprising therefore that the UK's Chartered Institute of Personnel and Development (CIPD) view organisations as the route to drive societal inclusion. Where the business case for diversity saw

26

growth and profits for organisations, the corporate social responsibility agenda (CSR) provided the means for organisations to donate towards worthy causes that aided building inclusion within communities in addition to supporting other economic and environmental initiatives.

Not all organisations value diversity in the same way and on seeing the sudden explosion of dark skin representation on television advertisements, the cynic in me wondered whether these organisations were truly inclusive. Were pay inequality or segmentation in existence within these structures? Had draconian attitudes, systems and practices that once perpetuated a culture of exclusion, been modernised? The public images through advertisements implied that these organisations either valued diversity or the black pound. There are ways in which these values may become known for all to see.

Corporate 'Lip Service'

Whilst being interviewed for a Human Resource role in a global organisation, I commented about the organisation's equality commitment found on their website which had impressed me. Their student sponsorship scheme was a great contribution to levelling up diverse groups and curious to learn more I asked whether such initiative was in operation in the UK, as it had not been evident on their website. The interview panel were suddenly more interested in what I presume were specks of dust on their desks rather than responding to my question. After a while of realising that I had no intention of disconnecting from the web call, they eventually looked up at me and replied, *'It's only in America.'*

Now, I appreciate that the interviewers may have been suffering from interview exhaustion, or they may have felt that discussing all the great initiatives the UK group had to offer would have taken too long a time to disclose. However, I expected more of a response, even something about the general equality groups they may have had in operation, but I got nothing. The real disappointment was that the location of organisation's multi storey offices where the job was based, is a stone's throw away from numerous universities and further educational establishments.

Whilst the support to students is extremely positive and potentially beneficial to those graduates who could potentially have a good start in a prestigious organisation, the initiative was not universally applied. In the UK, many large organisations have established equality groups amongst other initiatives that reflect their engagement and commitment to employees and

28

other stakeholders. However, this organisation appeared to have made a 'one of' gesture because of a public outcry, which becomes nothing more than a point scoring exercise.

Jumping on the Band Waggon

The point scoring 'one of' gesture may also be perceived as jumping on the bandwagon, another means of profitable gain. An advertisement that I came across on a social webpage glorified by a senior manager of a global organisation, showed in large print the words *'The reason we didn't make just one sports bra.'* Surrounding the caption were dozens of pictures of bare breasted women of all ethnicities, shapes, and sizes.

Recalling AIDA from my days as a business student, the advert most definitely grabbed my attention but there was certainly no interest, desire nor action to drive me to purchase the item in my skin colour. Ignoring the backward slide and offensive two finger salute to female activism, this organisation was proudly announcing its ability to now provide sports bras in various skin tone colours.

In fact, the possibility had always existed given that they sold multi coloured attire around the world, but it had merely chosen not to provide this service sooner. It therefore made sense that the organisation's actions were perceived as jumping on the bandwagon of the emotive circumstances, which made the advert another meaningless gesture. Simply notifying consumers of the new product range in an inoffensive manner would have been more advantageous. It serves as a reminder for organisations to be more mindful of the messages they convey publicly as they do portray their internal values.

Double Standards aka *'Dem damm wutless'* My Dad.

Double standards have become such a common theme in society that morality has lost its purpose. Articulation of one thing but acting on something else or not at all was a daily theme in the mismanagement of the UK's Covid-19 pandemic. Utilising British organisations to replenish personal protection equipment (PPE) stocks that the government had failed to update several months prior to the onslaught of the virus, would have been logical and would have minimised the use of the furlough scheme. Instead, crucial time was wasted and millions or billions of public monies was spent on unfit PPE stocks purchased abroad that were left buried in UK shipyards whilst countless precious lives were being lost.

We were all appreciative of the pharmaceutical companies producing large quantities of vaccines to mitigate and protect the world population from the devastating effects of the virus. The additional commitment of donating a percentage of their product to poorer nations, largely in the African continent, was a gesture which people valued, especially when hearing that no one was safe unless the world population was vaccinated. To then learn that this commitment was not upheld by a pharmaceutical organisation that had chosen instead to focus on amassing a financial fortune, was both shocking and disappointing.

When consideration is given to the lip service, the meaningless gestures or the double standards displayed publicly by organisations, it reinforces a necessity to assert one's choice of acceptance or rejection of what is being offered to the public.

The choice provided to me to have a Covid booster jab produced by the pharmaceutical company mentioned above was immediately rejected. In the same manner, I choose not to purchase brands that claim to be Caribbean produced when they are made in a basement somewhere in the UK. Neither will I purchase products from an organisation whose CEO representative rants racist abuse at its online customers. Nor will I shop in a store where the owner discounts the cost of a product that I have just purchased to his next customer because they share an ethnic origin. I am just one person asserting my choice based on my observations and experience so imagine the impact

31

to organisations if millions or billions of dark skin people responded in the same manner. This is not an impossibility given the use of social media at the public's disposal that enables the information sharing of such unethical practices.

Corporate Commitment

The success of a product or a service sold in the marketplace, is the result of the dedication, the commitment, and the contribution of key senior members of the organisation. The same level of drive and determination is a necessary requirement to affect the culture change that embeds inclusion within organisations. Where senior members are non-compliant or dismissive of such commitments, then it would be reasonable, in my opinion, for them to relinquish their position for a worthier replacement skilled in upholding the organisation's values.

The most welcomed news announced by a former Health Minister on receipt of yet another commissioned equality report about the failures in a NHS trust, was that reform of the service was essential to remove its racist culture. They recommended the removal of the existing leadership who were deemed responsible for the toxic culture that had contributed to the diminished standards within the service. It was the most constructive statement I had heard from a representative of the Government in such a very long time.

Organisations typically reform and rebrand their services or products by getting rid of the old and outdated to replace it with the modern and more effective solutions to achieve success. Why then is it difficult to apply the same principles to address the inequality within its structures so that the illusion of inclusion is removed? Reviewing and reforming the systems and practices that restrict, deny and segment dark skin employees in the workplace is not so challenging, especially where organisations have previously carried out the foundation work. The access to employment, development opportunities, pay benefits and formal procedures enacted are the areas to begin the review process.

What organisations tend to overlook when updating these processes, however, is the practices adopted by those employees accountable and entrusted with the responsibilities for maintaining the employment relationship and an inclusive work environment. Impact assessing this management activity may enlighten organisations to the possible causes for why inclusion may not be working within its structures. Do not be surprised once this activity is undertaken, to uncover another empire or two operating within.

The introduction of the UK's updated equality laws and the Race Equality Scheme following the biased investigation into the murder of Stephen Lawrence, brought what I had hoped would be better treatment within society and in the workplace, towards dark skin people. The shameful reality is that very little has changed aside from the increased exposures of the obtuse level of the mistreatment. Public organisations in the UK have been humiliated by the reporting of continual disproportionate standards shown towards its dark skin workforce and service users. Some commercial organisations on the other hand, appear to have highjacked emotive events with empty or one-off gestures. Although these are general observations, praise and recognition must be given to those organisations who are and continue to be proactive and progressive with diversity within their workforce.

CHAPTER 3

The Nature of Racism

As a youngster the prejudices of other people became my prejudices for a short time at least, because I did not know any better and as a child, I was learning from other people who no doubt formed biases based on their own personal experiences. This changed in time where the views and opinions of others were replaced with those opinions that I formed for myself. These opinions were not determined by a person's skin colour but by their character and behaviour towards me. Treat others the same way that you would like to be treated was my mother's guidance and is a rule that governs me today. I am sure that I do not stand alone in never judging a book by its cover and yet the prejudices formed about dark skin people, particularly black people are laughable because anything else would make them true.

For example, the stereotypical view of my skin colour would define me as an aggressive and violent, strong minded yet docile, mentally inferior, lazy, and physically and emotionally unevolved person, to name but a few labels. It would be possible to become aggressive and turn to violent if my life or those of

35

my loved ones were constantly threatened. Strong mindedness is nothing more than determination and being docile and lazy is a must when having a day off work so that my brain has a rest from dealing with challenging egomaniacs.

Mental inferiority, I must raise my hand to because I cannot understand the obsession with reality television or allowing my thoughts or my life to be controlled by all things digital/artificially intelligent. Placing goggles over the eyes to pretend to live and play in an alternate universe or indeed to live on another planet when mother earth is so breathtakingly beautiful, has me completely baffled. May I suggest that those who are committed to making space travel and living a reality for the Elysium elite, that they redirect their energies towards Jupiter or Venus as I understand the climate there is much warmer than on the Moon.

As for being physically and mentally unevolved, well I have simply learnt to love the human being that I am including my limitations. I am not perfect because I have strengths and weaknesses both mentally and physically just like every living person on the planet, that is not borne out of having a different skin colour.

Whilst reading the book '*White Privilege*' by Paula S Rothenberg, I was suddenly propelled into a dormant childhood memory of being surrounded by a group of white skin children while they chanted a rhyme. It was a forgotten experience but to ensure that it had not been a figment of my imagination, I asked a couple of my siblings about the rhyme, and I received the confirmation that I did not always have my head up in the clouds or in some adult magazine (Woman's Own!!).

The rhyme reflected the hierarchical levels of acceptability based upon the social construct of skin colour. I believe it was the chapter by James E Barrett and David Roediger '*How White People Became White*' that triggered the memory and made me reflect upon what was perceived to be true some decades ago, appearing to remain true today. The rhyme is....

> '*If you are white, you are alright.*
> *If you are yellow, you are mellow.*
> *If you are brown, stick around.*
> *If you are black, stay back.*'

I do not know its origins and do not care to know, but it clearly continues to reinforce racist behaviours, whether overtly or covertly. For me, it explained why people whose skin colour are socially categorised as black continue to experience challenges that prevent their progression in life. Let us reflect upon my observations of this colour hierarchy in operation.

If you are White….

The privileges of whiteness are discussed in the White Privilege book, explaining how the USA viewed the various ethnicities around the world that were progressively accepted and assimilated into the colour grouping of whiteness. In Europe, colonialism achieved the same purpose where concerted efforts maintained a preference towards light than dark skin people. It is interesting that only a few decades ago, the people of Ireland were once aligned with black people and dogs in the unwanted social group within the UK, proving that social acceptance is possible.

White skin colour group is the current benchmark to which all other skin colours are compared in all sectors of life. The eternal list of this 'like me' middleclass, blond hair, blue eyed male stereotype makes the value of acceptance into this skin colour group an illusion. Differences of physique, nationalities, ethnicities, cultures, and values makes this skin colour grouping no different to any others with its diverse mix.

However, the nature of racism is often viewed as the differences between white and black skin people. An example of this would be the appalling treatment of some white skin football fans towards the black England football players following the 2021 European Champions semi-finals match with France. Having once been an avid football fan in my younger years, it was always a disappointment to see the fans fighting after matches, which were commonly reported as hooliganism. Such behaviour was not restricted to homeland football teams, but to any opposing team of a different nationality whether the games were played at home or abroad. Whilst the white skin colour of fans may have been the common feature, their nationalities differed, which made the conduct towards each other, racism.

It was a shock to learn that after the centuries since emancipation, the last of the Government's bribe payment to former slave owners for the freedom of black slaves was paid in 2015. Take a moment to absorb this fact, that a portion of the tax contributions of every person made throughout their working lives since the abolition of the slave trade, was paid to former slave owners. Unfortunately, the economics of slave agreements are not restricted to this one activity. Trade agreements in the form of debts continues to shackle African countries to the USA, European countries, and private companies. Much of these loans consists of extortionate interest rates that restrains Africans in economic poverty, restricting their ability to rebuild their countries and provide adequate citizen support. The unshackling of this arrangement rests in the hands of institutions such as the International Monetary Fund, world banks and G7 countries who all appear reluctant to release their chains.

This may appear to be a reasonable course of action where a financial debt is owed, but the treatment towards African countries must be compared to Iceland. When in 2008, Iceland experienced economic turmoil and unable to pay its debts, the same institutions cancelled the country's debt and allowed them time to independently resolve their economic situation free from external influence. The most obvious difference in the treatment shown to Iceland when compared to Africa, is one of skin colour. One must wonder why the perceived most civilised and wealthy western countries are unable to survive without the continued pillaging of African resources and stand on their own two feet. Colonialism and Debt - Debt Justice. The Debt Justice and Guardian websites are just a few organisations providing

40

insightful information about the debts and with continued public support, we can only hope that more will be done to remove this modern-day shackle once and for all.

If you are Yellow......

All continents benefited from the enslavement of Africans and the mistreatment of other dark skin people in history and Asia is no different. The traditions of dark skin inferiority have been reported in more recent times from the Chinese students' riots objecting to African student university admissions in the 1980's, to the reporting of mistreatment towards dark skin people throughout the covid pandemic.

Reports by Human Rights Watch brought to my attention the mistreatment of Africans and African Americans residing in China. It seems the country's media reports accused black people of being responsible for the spread of the Covid-19 virus. The country responsible for this virus and its spread around the world, blames Africans for its cause. It was interesting to note how within a few decades that black people were once again being blamed for a virus that was killing off humanity.

This distain towards dark skin people extends into the employment arena where Chinese organisations may expressly exclude dark skin candidates when advertising vacancies. This leads me to question, for all this blatant racism towards black people, why are many African countries in partnership with the Chinese government to build African infrastructures worth billions of dollars? Interestingly, BBC Africa News reported in August 2022 that the Chinese government had proposed the removal of its loans to 17 African countries and to help build the African economies with the provision of food and imports etc. It is difficult to view this arrangement as nothing but another shackle of debt entrapment. Imagine African nations united in providing each other with constructive support to rebuild African economies. The restoration of countries to their precolonial empires, free from the manipulative influences of external forces. Now that would be a great vision to behold in my lifetime.

If you are Brown......

Even though the skin colours compare, there is no doubt that South Asians have benefited from the accomplishments of African and Caribbean descendants who fought for equal treatment and improved race relations. Where white skin control over black skin dominated economic and social sectors, brown skin colours have built local control over black through the essentials of foods and general services. Having an anti-black culture embedded by legacies of imperialism with colourism and a cultural caste system of a preference towards light skin tones, the relationship between black and brown has been a very mixed bag. However, the perceived relationship of brown skin and black skin is viewed by the other skin colours as one of sameness.

I recall reading an article reported in August 2015 by the Guardian news, about an African teacher who had been stabbed by an Asian student who had called the teacher the 'N' word several times before he acted. The head of the Muslim school and the local Member of Parliament both stated that the incident was not racially motivated because both teacher and pupil were Muslims and so they viewed colourism as the reason for the incident. The skin colours of the parties clearly differed which resulted in the verbal abuse directed at the teacher. The student's behaviour may be explained by their cultural upbringing that perceives darker skin colour people as inferior human beings. However, the fact remains that both parties involved in the incident did not share the same skin colour or nationality or ethnic origin and therefore, the actions of the student was one of racial hatred which for me was compounded by the overt act of racist name calling.

Much has been reported from media sources such as Human Rights Watch and the BBC on the human rights abuses of migrant workers in the Middle Eastern countries, especially prior to the build-up of the 2022 World Cup event in Qatar. Knowing that dark skin people from the African Continent were made to work in slave like conditions which included segregation, abusive treatment and the lack of safety equipment resulting in the loss of many lives, made me personally unable to watch the football event. The 'Kafala' sponsorship system that legally binds the employer to the worker they sponsored no doubt would have played a key role in the shackling of the parties in this life-threatening form of employment. Having material and financial wealth, does not earn a human being the right to destroy the life of another.

If you are Black....

There is no doubt that this skin colour is supremely different when compared to the other skin colours. Distinguishable traditionally by the darker skin tones hence being referenced as black, the physical difference also includes the hair, nose, and lips. The uniqueness of black is such that other skin colours continue to demonise and devalue its existence so that they may gain ownership of all things black to repurpose as their own.

United by our African heritage, cultural differences exist between those born in Africa to those born in the Caribbean, to those born in the UK or the USA or anywhere else in the world. Sharing the black skin colour collectively unites us, as does our shared values and traditions but colourism is a toxin that also permeates through this skin colour group. Another toxin is polarisation which is often politicised when comparisons are made between Caribbean and African descendants regarding lifestyles or educational attainment for example. Such effort truly serves no purpose given the existing anti-black attitudes of the other skin colours towards all thing black.

There was a time when it was perceived that a drop of black blood within the mixing of different ethnicities placed a person in the category of black, irrespective of the colour tone of their skin. The film, '*Imitation of Life*', with Lana Turner and Juanita Moore who plays the mother of a child of mixed ethnicities, comes to mind. Whilst these views have now changed, the acceptance of black remains controversial. For example, the

45

equality monitoring forms which are the tools for assessing the ethnicities within the UK population, distinguishes two ethnicities by skin colour and not others. Yet I noted today when completing a monitoring form that white British have its tick box of belonging, but none existed for black British, only the choice option of the Caribbean or Africa. Am I not a black British citizen? I was born and currently live in England and whilst I am extremely proud of my ancestry, I cannot help but wonder what it must take for a black person to be acknowledged and accepted as British?

Looking at the blossoming branches of the family tree where I belong, there are different skin colours that are members. They are not defined by white, black, and all the colour shades in-between, but by the names of brother, nieces, nephews, great nieces, and nephews. When I reflect on my own heritage, there are many ethnicities mixed in my bloodline, which is to be expected having Jamaican parents and the history that lies within. My big sis has already populated a great deal of my mother's family tree which I often joke will take her back to anatomical Eve, if all our ancestral bloodline records existed. Having started my father's side of the tree, I hope to resume the project with family members sometime soon to see where it leads.

My dad often spoke of his grandfather Charlie and his sister Jerusa visiting to play with him when a child, and he remembered his grandfather's big red hair and big blue eyes. I have yet to discover whether this bloodline link is true but the tinges of blue in the iris of my father's eyes were more noticeable as he got older, as is the case with many people of the same ethnic background. The iris colour changes may have been the result of a medical condition, but I prefer to view it as part the ancestral blood line which for me makes this social obsession with skin colour ridiculous.

Do you get it? The malicious conscious bias towards skin colour was socially constructed for reasons of capitalism and control. This evil survives only to retain a distorted perspective of superiority. The acceptance of difference and the inclusion of difference is a natural construct of mother earth that seeks replenishment and not the destruction of her natural gifts.

CHAPTER 4

The Classes of Racism

Racism created a social hierarchy based on skin colour, but we cannot ignore that a similar structure exists that was founded on a perceived structure of wealth. The notion of wealth is subjective, but we are taught, or rather I was taught from an early age that knowledge enabled a person to achieve their wealth and a social status in life. Competitiveness was the driving force that enabled a person to succeed using their talents and would aid in the achievement of a status and financial wealth within organisations. It made sense to me then, having a religious upbringing, that those individuals who lacked the capacity to accomplish such a status through honourable means and resorted to deviant and backstabbing tactics to achieve their ambitions in life, would meet their victims on the downward trajectory to the cesspool.

Class System

One of my favourite books read at my secondary school of Archbishop Masterson Roman Catholic School, was *'An Inspector Calls'* by JB Priestly. A 1912 play about the class system in British society was turned into a film in 1946 starring one of my favourite Ealing actors, Alistair Sims. It was a film that resonated because it focused on the behaviours and actions of privilege people towards a working-class woman. This powerful piece of literature forces the characters to reflect upon their own actions and behaviours towards a vulnerable person. The police inspector who represents consciousness, strips away their dignity in the most considered way, in the search for a soul.

The modern class structure has seen an increase of levels due to the technology sector creating more billionaires that there are now appears to be seven levels to its structure. Focusing on a few of the categories, the play introduces us to seven key characters whose social status and personality traits are shown below.

The play shows us the condescension of a perceived superior group of people over another. Watch the black and white film and tell me that the ending does not disrupt your psyche.

Characters	Status	Personality Trait
Mr Birling	Middle Class	Authoritarian business owner and a former Lord Mayor who has higher aspirations. Narrow minded, his rule is law and condescends to all who are not of an equal status.
Mrs Birling	Upper Middle Class	Although married beneath their social status, a shared condescension unites. Perceive themself a role model to which others should aspire. Charitable projects provide a self-fulfilling purpose of inflating their status.
Gerald Croft	Upper Class / Aristocrat	The fiancé from an affluent family, who refuses to engage with any status below middle class, unless to their own advantage.
Sheila Birling	Middle Class	Views parent's attitudes as draconian and will publicly advocate for the new and modern approaches but finds comfort in the old traditions.
Eric Birling	Middle Class	Liberal and indifferent to the class structure, objects to draconian lifestyles and attitudes.
Inspector Poole	Middle Class	Consciousness: Intuitive and uses discernment to find the truth of a situation. The objective bystander.
Eva Smith.	Working Class	Compassionate and selfless advocate of fairness. Challenged and judged by those deemed her superiors

Race System

When considering the types of discrimination to apply to the class structure, it was natural to use the definitions identified by Benokraitis and Feagin (1995) contained in Sonia Liff's academic paper on diversity. These forms of discrimination are:

Overt Discrimination

In the UK overt discrimination is aligned with direct discrimination whereas in the USA, the term used is associative discrimination. The discriminatory conduct is defined as the direct actions and decisions taken by one person against another because of their skin colour. An example of this would be the social media racist abuse towards the three dark skin England football players as mentioned earlier. Another workplace example of overt discrimination typically occurs in recruitment and selection processes where candidates with non-traditional first or surnames are deselected from the candidate pool.

Subtle Discrimination

Known as indirect discrimination in the UK or perceptive discrimination in the USA. These are the acts or behaviours that are visible and may not be viewed as intentional because they are seen as normal. Remaining with recruitment and selection, an example of subtle discrimination would be a job advertisement for a general job stipulating either a professional qualification or a high pass grade as a minimum requirement. Such restrictions may deter or limit the applications of dark skin candidates who may have the qualification but not to the required grade level or who may have comparable years of practical experience in the role but no formal qualification.

Covert Discrimination

Covert discrimination is not dissimilar to the malicious and vexatious behaviours that UK legislation recognises in the conduct of individuals who discriminate. These are the actions and behaviours that are hidden and are intended to cause great harm. Again, an example within recruitment process is those high scoring dark skin candidates who are denied the offer of employment due to a perceived 'fit' concern of panel members.

Another example is the events that occurred during the Formulae One 2021 world championship race, which I watched from the comfort of my home. I wanted to see my hero win his eighth world championship title and I had my rum punch drink at the ready. The car crash on the final lap could not have been expected, although it almost felt orchestrated given the events that followed. The decision makers empowered to ensure the adherence of the established track rules known to all drivers, suddenly change the rules towards the end of the race. This act in my opinion, served only one purpose, which was to deny my hero his crown.

There was no justification for the rule change, not even the views that I heard some of the sports presenters announce to the watching audience that it was about entertaining the fans. No, that was not an acceptable reason and was simply a subjective viewpoint. The fact remains that established rules were manipulated by biased decision makers which caused a detriment that was clearly maliciously intended to deny my hero his deserved crown. No matter the sector, racism is racism.

Now, changing the dynamics slightly, let us consider the characters from 'An Inspector Calls' from the perspective of racism.

Character	Status	Personality Trait
Mr Birling	Overt Racist	The *'Like Me'* racist only engages with those who share their skin colour and views difference as inferior to be controlled and disempowered so that it remains subservient.
Mrs Birling	Overt/Covert Racist	The *'I Don't Care What You Have, I Don't Want It'* racist, uses acquired platforms to promote their hate agenda, often hidden behind egotistical saviour activities to increase their social status.
Gerald Croft	Overt Racist	The *'You Are Not Like the Others'* racist are the players who create illusions with their selective saviour tendencies, for personal gain.
Sheila Birling	Subtle Racist	The *'I Have a Friend Who Is Black'* racist, abhors outdated attitudes and its privileges when not used as a comfort blanket. A champion for equality, although real commitment only occurs when personally impacted by a disadvantage.
Eric Birling	Anti-Racist	Values difference and judges a person not by their skin colour but by their character.
Inspector Poole	Anti-Racist	Consciousness: Challenges racist views and behaviours.
Eva Smith	Dark Skin Victim	Denied the rights to life due to a toxic and idiotic social perception of inferiority attachment to skin colour.

Views may differ in this simplified definition of the traits and categorisation of classism and racism and that is perfectly acceptable. We will all have differing views that will be born out of our different life experiences, just like those of Eva Smith with each member of the Birling family. The important point is the discourse that follows and to enjoy the debate as some readers may uncomfortably identify with one or more of the characters outlined above.

The lesson and possibly the challenge is the ability to align oneself to the Inspector by playing devil's advocate before making important decisions although it is recognised that people have short memories and may revert to patterns of unethical conduct.

All actions have consequences but whether the action would be repeated if people foresaw the consequences of their actions is a question that can only be answered individually. Regret is a powerful emotion that torments the soul when there is a failure to think logically before acting towards someone or something. Hence the guidance of placing oneself into the shoes of the other person, before making any decisions.

CHAPTER 5

What Equality?

The Universal Declaration of Human Rights 1948 was formulated following the second world war to bring international peace to the world. It states that every person is entitled to all rights and freedom '*without distinction of any kind, such as race, colour, sex, language, religion, political or other opinion, national or social origin, property, birth or status.*' However, it was the proactive stance of the 1960s Black Power movement that brought about noticeable changes in social attitudes towards black people.

The UK was the first European country to recognise the need for social change with the introduction of the Race Relations Act 1965 that prohibited discrimination in public places. Workplace discrimination remained acceptable in the UK until further changes in the law introduced direct race discrimination 1968. Indirect discrimination joined the team in 1976 which prohibited the provision, criteria or practice that may be equally applied to all people but disadvantaged a black individual or group. It took for Lord MacPherson's report into the metropolitan police service's biased investigation into the murder of black teenager Stephen Lawrence in 1999, for the legislation to be amended in 2000. The new changes acknowledged the existence of institutional racism in public services and imposed requirements on these institutions to remove inequality both internally and externally when providing a service.

Race relations is just one of the golden nuggets attached to the golden padlock of human rights protection, alongside other distinctions that the UK law recognises as protected characteristics. Within the workplace, equal opportunities policies and strategies were created to focus on the inequality caused to employees of different social groups. As a young dark skin female, my experience and understanding of equal opportunity meant getting over the threshold of the employing organisation to secure employment. Beyond this point, equal treatment would be a frequent challenge whenever I dared to question the reason for my being given less than my colleagues. When equal opportunity strategies shifted towards the principle of valuing individuality and cultural differences, the optimist in me welcomed the change.

57

Organisations saw the social and commercial benefits that a diverse workforce could achieve, opening themselves to global customers and increased profit margins. Social and economic growth occurred for many commercial organisations, but public organisations transformed at a much slower pace. The introduction of the race equality scheme injected new possibilities and aspirations into these structures. Constructive processes for removing inequality that dissected business functions to remove draconian processes to be replaced with modern inclusive approaches, were measures that the public desperately sought. Regrettably the incentive for change and removing barriers became a diminishing lack lustre process that appeared to be dumped on the bathroom floor of cost cutting and restructure programmes.

Despite the explicit duty contained in equality law, that is; to eliminate all forms of discrimination, to advance equality of opportunity and to foster good relations between people, many public organisations appear to have failed in its compliance. The public reports seem never ending with medical, ambulance, fire service and more police service reports exposing the extent of internal racist behaviours. There is no doubt that despite the extremely disturbing reports on the conduct of some of its officers, the newly appointed London Metropolitan Police Commissioner appears determined to cleanse the service of its destructive behaviours. Their action towards rebuilding public confidence is exactly what other Commissioners and leaders of public services need to adopt. I only hope that the racism within these institutions is not once again marginalised or overlooked in the process of these service transformations.

Cost cutting measures imposed by the ministerial members of the government cannot be ignored as one of the reasons for the diminishing standards within public institutions in the past decade or so. Budget reductions leading to the restructures and the reprioritisation of business objectives are often the excuses given for equality strategies losing their purpose. However, had best practices been properly embedded within these structures from the outset, equality would not have died or have been compromised, surely? As evidenced by the new Police Commissioner's conduct, the problem is not the strategy, but those accountable for its deliverance.

Recalling my time spent as a member of an equality group reviewing an organisation's policies, there was much debate about not wanting the project to become just a tick box exercise. Yet, this was a crucial step to establish a foundation upon which the organisation could build and improve its business functions and services. As with many public organisations, the initial positive drive of establishing employee groups, conducting training sessions, updating functions in the employment cycle, and looking at creative ways to improve service delivery, in time began to lose momentum.

On reviewing progress of the organisation's equality strategy a few years later, equality had become insignificant. The organisation had undergone a couple of restructures and the inadequate monitoring data reflected the nonchalant attitude of its leader. Sadly, this meant that those earlier identified barriers that restricted dark skin employees from developing and progressing with the workplace, remained in situ.

Conversely, I was fortunate to have worked alongside a diversity manager who was passionately driven to improve equality standards within their organisation through proactive stakeholder engagement activities. They were extremely effective in their work and so it was disappointing to learn a year or so later that a bullying senior manager had ousted the diversity manager from their role and kicked equality into the basement.

New Initiatives

The CIPD website promotes new initiatives encouraging organisations to move towards an anti-racist structure, picking up the slack where those leaders responsible for this social change of inclusion have failed to deliver.

Mutual mentoring is one such concept to guide leaders of organisations towards a more informed understanding of racism by mentoring dark skin employees. This approach is seen to enable managers to gain a better understanding of the disadvantages experienced by dark skin employees, whilst raising their profile in the workplace.

Whilst such an initiative has positive intentions, it makes me uncomfortable knowing that such arrangements would make any employee uncomfortable, never mind a dark skin employee. Feeling pressured into disclosing personal and often painful experiences just to satisfy another employee's curiosity places an unnecessary psychological burden on the dark skin employee. It is my view that such a burden is one that dark skin employees can do without. There are enough stresses which an employee must contend with daily and so placing emphasis on their skin colour, their difference, in an environment where they differ to the dominant workforce, is not helpful.

61

Having a 'safe space' to have these disclosure conversations is not what dark skin people seek when entering the employment arena. They merely want to be treated the same as any other member of the workforce. Any safe spaces for confidential conversations should be encouraged for the disclosure of any acts of unfair treatment that prompts immediate management action, rather than be swept under the office carpet.

Another concept is Allyship which the CIPD's Race on Equality Charter promotes by encouraging the dominant group in the organisation to be proactive in removing inequality by advancing the interests of dark skin employees. This may possibly mean fighting a workplace cause on behalf of the dark skin employee whenever the need arises. Would this action be required because the dark skin employee does not have a voice, cannot be understood or would it be because they are not listened to? It is likely to be the latter in which case how can meritocracy be achieved when a dark skin employee achieves progression in their career through piggybacking off the championing of a dominant group employee? Where is the credibility in such actions? This can only serve to bolster the status of one employee whilst further diminishing the abilities and integrity of another.

Championing a dark skin employee does not address the problem of not being listened to and only maintains a saviour complex of helping the dark skin employees rather than acknowledging their capabilities and addressing the problem causing barrier. Dark skin employees do not seek a different or preferential treatment, but the same treatment as other privileged employees in the workplace.

Where organisations have adopted these initiatives and they are proven to be a success, then any published evidence will go some way into providing guidance to other organisations. The best practices to adopt to achieve the goal of an inclusive representative workforce, would be most welcomed for all dark skin employees.

Coalition - The Way Forward?

'What White People Can Do Next from Allyship to Coalition' by Emma Dabiri, brings forth a concept coined in the USA of coalition that creates inclusion based on a common ground. This concept focuses on creating alliances between the social groups with protected characteristics who share similar challenges. Its purpose was originally seen as a means for

achieving greater social justice through support programmes that addressed social and economic poverty, whilst enabling people to level up.

Coalition seems to make sense when you consider the disproportionalities that are occurring in society today, whether in wealth distribution, employment, education even environmental issues. Working in alliance with other vulnerable groups to bring about fair treatment makes sense, but is that not the responsibility of governments around the world? (It is a rhetorical question). One could argue that coalition of sorts has occurred in organisations under the umbrella of corporate social responsibilities, yet it seems possible that more could be achieved to level up social sectors. For example, it was admirable to see during the Covid 19 pandemic lockdowns that some organisations donated unused laptops to schools around the country to enable children, especially in deprived communities, to continue with their education online. Embedding such practices where practicable enhances an organisation's reputation than any one-off gesture could.

The amalgamation of the UK's individual discrimination legislations governing those areas of protected characteristics into a single Equality Act can be perceived as a step towards the alliance principles. However, its application into the workplace may prove difficult given that each protected characteristics have different strands and complex challenges. Having a sound understanding of the depth and breadth of each area would be a steep undertaking, which is why the concept of coalition needs to be placed firmly at the doors of a competent government. By following the coalition principles aimed to rebuild an economy, a levelling up of the socially disadvantaged may well yet be achieved.

Intersectionality

Being not so dissimilar to coalition, intersectionality is the term that recognises that the disadvantages experienced by people are not confined to one social grouping defined by the equality law, but by multiple groupings which also takes account of social and economic factors.

The life experiences of a dark skin person that led them to become an employee in the organisation may completely differ or be like a white skin person. Not every person is born into privilege, or receives a first-class education, or grew up in a stable home. Each person will have overcome every day challenges walking on their life's path to fulfil their personal ambitions, developing skills and knowledge that ultimately leads them to their place of employment. The disadvantages experienced in the workplace by the employee because of one or more protected characteristic, is not because of their privately lived experiences. The disadvantages experienced in the workplace are the result of the attitudes and actions of other employees, or the established policies and practices that prevents dark skin employees from receiving fair and equal treatment.

Equality Next Steps

Having thought about the next steps and possible alternate solutions to equality initiatives in the workplace, I could find no answer. My thoughts kept returning to the simple fact that dark skin employees do not seek to be treated more nor less favourably than the dominant employee group. Any newly suggested initiative would continue to boost a superhero culture that implied all dark skin employees were incompetent or incapable of achieving on their own merit, which is far from the truth.

Equality initiatives such as mutual mentoring or allyship seems to serve the purpose of inflating the egos of senior participants rather than them addressing the root causes of inequality within the organisation. Acceptance of difference and being the recipient of equal treatment would hold greater value and earn commitment. Whether or not organisations have effective equality strategies in place, it would be worthwhile reviewing those existing business activities and staffing data to identify the barriers towards inclusion that may have been overlooked. The following chapters will provide examples of some areas for consideration which may result in the updating of current practices, retaining the good, whilst eliminating the bad. This will help to create the solid foundations for equality to transform, rather than it being an illusion.

Do you get it? Replacing an old skin with the new is superficial and creates an illusion that avoids the necessary deep dive to address the barriers impacting upon the inclusion of dark skin employees within the workplace.

CHAPTER 6

~~Not~~ 'Like Me' Syndrome

Entering a new work environment can be a daunting experience for any person as there is an expectation that new entrants leave their identities at home and conform to a new culture. There are many rules to navigate that dictate conformity and acceptance into the new environment. From the unwritten rules of wearing a uniform in the form of a suit or a smart dress to reflect professionalism and sameness, to abiding by the written rules and procedures so that individualism is replaced with a collective compliance. It implied that you would provide a fair days work to receive a fair day's pay and the parties will trust each other.

The expectations appear limitless, for example being polite and cordial towards all colleagues and stakeholders and utilising developed professional skills effectively, ensuring that you add value to the business aims. Also, the relinquishing of ownership of your specialist knowledge and ideas to the new employer, all for the sake of acceptance, and getting paid. Admittedly this is a brief one-sided perspective of some elements of the employment contract that exists between organisations and employees.

All organisations claim to be different with having their own identities, ethos, and aspirations that they expect employees to share or adopt and yet on closer inspection, the cultures within these organisations are not so dissimilar. Profit driven or not, the employees' efforts appear to benefit none other than those senior members sat at the high table, (sorry but I'm a John Wick fan!!) and not those employees who sit at the lower echelons who are often the creators, developers, and the drivers of the organisation's initiatives.

Starting a new job or a new collaboration with an organisation whilst an exciting new beginning, is also one that determines whether you will fit into your new work environment. How you look, how you speak, how you interact with the team, how you effectively apply your skills and all the rest of it will determine whether you are offered the red pill or the blue pill to success. (Yes, I'm a Matrix fan too!). Yet a dark skin employee knows only too well that there will be other workplace challenges to overcome, not merely because of working alongside a workforce that do not share their skin colour. No, the challenge is the expectation of a complete transformation where the dark skin employee is required to change into a white skin employee for the sake of sameness.

69

Behaviour

There is a requirement that you share some level of similarity to those that you work with, whether at departmental or senior level. These similarities must be shared through a collective criterion of gender, qualifications, values, and ways of behaving, which achieves a purpose of gaining the acceptance of your co-workers so as not to be treated differently.

When reflecting upon starting a new job in a new environment, I laugh at how I transitioned from essentially a tea drinker into an alcoholic, almost. My new white skin colleagues liked to have a drink after work and always invited me to join them, not wanting me to feel alone or uncomfortable. The more they asked, the more I felt pressured into joining them because I did not want to feel excluded from the team. What I had not realised was that they had already accepted me and saw me as a respected member of the team. I should not have felt compelled to join them after work on a Friday evening, or at lunchtimes for a drink or two or more. It was an experience finding myself progress from a sweet sparling white wine drinker to a deep robust red wine before progressing to only having a palate for strong beers.

Many organisations whether knowingly or not, can place unnecessary pressures upon employees to attend events that are induction rituals into team memberships. There have been many instances where '*No Thanks*' became my automated response simply because I had no interest in listening to the personal problems, the latest dietary fads, or the latest notch achieved on the bedpost of work colleagues.

Red Flag: A refusal to participate in social events should not be interpreted as not wanting to be a part of the team or an inability to do a job well. It just means that there are other priorities outside of the workplace hours requiring attention so do not label dark skin employees as unsociable, strange, or lacking in commitment.

Hair

Hair style is another of the unspoken rules which ideally should be conservative and appropriate to fit with the other colleagues in the organisation. Loosely interpreted as role modelling a senior staff member, otherwise you may be met with derisory looks or flippant remarks. But what happens when no one has hair like mine? You make sure that your hair is either tied back or has neat hair extensions. Permed hair from a chemically infused fragrant substance designed to kill off the

71

black woman, must be styled in such a way that is unnoticeable so that you assimilate into the corporate norm. The general rule for afros is an absolute no! Not allowed, please!! So, to avoid any paper spit balls speckling the hair, the precious 'fro is controlled with a hot press comb so that your hair looks as good as but not better than your white skin colleagues.

Yet, it never ceases to amaze how colleagues who see you daily during the working week can believe in the impossibility of the 10-inch hair growth over a weekend. Changing up the hair style with braid extensions always provokes at least one person to approach you from behind to touch your new hair style. With a forward-facing approach you are at least be prepared as you make eye contact with the inquisitive colleague and see the glazed look of amazement incoming. You see the arm reaching out that you know what's coming next and can do a sidestep or turn your head slightly so that a complete avoidance occurs of the touching of your new fresh hair braids with those crusty hands that smothered the posterior when exiting the toilet moments earlier.

A rear attack is the one that is unavoidable because you are usually consumed in your work at your desk or worse still, in deep discussion on a call, that you are utterly and completely vulnerable to the unannounced prey. An announcement of *'Ooooh, is that your hair?'* followed by a heavy palm slapping your crown before sliding down the nape of your neck and onwards, fingers twiddling in and out of as many braids that can be touched. This is not a seductive caress or the gently repositioning of an out of place braid. No, it's the rough stroking of a dog or the quick drying of hands when the toilets have run out of paper towels. Reactions to such offence would normally result in the exchange of some bad words but in the workplace, it is usually a firm but polite *'Please don't touch my hair'*. Yet it is the dark skin employee who must be mindful of how they express themselves to avoid being labelled with having an attitude when they are the ones who have just been assaulted.

Red Flag: *'Your hair is your beauty'* are the precious words of my mom. It is versatile, it is unique and like Samson, it is strong. So irrespective of how it is styled, please, don't ever touch my hair!

Dress

The clothing must not be too brightly coloured as you will stand out and may be accused of bringing the colourful traditions of carnival into the workplace. Thankfully, modern clothing designers have created colourful uniforms deemed acceptable for the workplace that your unique style of dress is becoming more acceptable. But be warned that remarks from your fellow colleagues of '*Ooh that's different*', whilst stroking your multi-coloured blouse without your permission, may still occur.... isn't that sexual assault?!!

Communication

The spoken language in business must be that of the Queen's English because speaking any other English is considered a foreign language or too common for use in the organisation that you now represent. Lord help those who have an accent, express any patois, or speak any kind of foreign in the workspace because you will be looked upon as if you had expressed the noisiest and smelliest fart that those standing nearest to you will jump aside in complete horror and disgust.

Admittedly, interpretation can become a two-way problem. Dark skin employees must learn to decipher languages and be telepathic when seeking answers to a query. For example, where a detailed step by step explanation may be patiently communicated to those who share a skin colour, a terse *'Just get on with it'* or a cryptic response is given to dark skin employees. A relative of mine likens the cryptic response experience to the Bake-Off's technical challenge bake, where essential steps in the challenge are omitted, that contestants can only guess what they might be and hope for a decent outcome.

Communications of flippant, condescending, or bitchy remarks when seeking advice is often aimed to demean instead of providing a language of encouragement and support. A former manager would often make the comments *'You are not always right but you are wrong again'* whenever I sought their advice on a task. It may have been a strapline from a favourite comedian, I am not sure, but as the only dark skin employee in the team who seemed to be the only recipient of these remarks, I took exception to it. On hearing these words once too often, I responded with *'Yes sir massah, I's be a good n***a massah!'*. Now being a liberal minded person, the manager understandably took offence at my retort, but they had failed to have any regard for the impact of their words, which should have encouraged rather than demean a team member. Knowingly or not, their remarks were a constant putdown and failed to provide the constructive critique that I sought from a manager and so their perspective required a disruption. Suffice to say those comments were never made again, although I would occasionally say *'Yes massah'* if they made any condescending remarks or just generally whenever they were annoying.

Red Flag: Telepathy is not gifted to most people, unlike the ability to convey clear and constructive communications.

Intelligence

It should be no surprise that many people of all ethnicities who enter employment have had and continue to have some form of education. Levels of intelligence will differ because we are all different and our educational experiences are different. The display of intelligence should be welcomed and not be a cause of upset that you become the recipient of sarcastic remarks of *'Oh, I didn't realise you had a brain'* on completing a complex business project. Intelligence does not give permission to downright overload a dark skin person with work without the curtesy of any prior discussion. Objections to such acts are usually met with *'Oh you can do it'* as if championing a development cause. This frustrates to the core because you know exactly what you are capable of and yes you can do it, but so too can the administrative team whose responsibilities have just been handed to you.

Assimilation into the team is important and so hiding capabilities may become the norm so that others are not intimidated by the knowledge or versatile talents of their dark skin colleague, whilst they adapt to seeing difference in their working day.

Red Flag: Competencies that add value to achieving business goals should not be diminished or belittled, but positively utilised.

Misconduct

It is reasonable to expect to have a little informal chat whenever a misstep occurs in the line of duty so that the necessary lessons are learnt. Not so when the expectation of compliance requires a dark skin employee to be *'whiter than white'* because any deviation will result in the holy book of rules being thrown at you in the sacred name of *'aggressive behaviour'*. Yet it is amazing to suddenly find yourself as the recipient of formal disciplinary action because you asked the simple question of whether someone liked their coffee black.

It may sound silly, but accusations of aggression are not uncommon and are usually the result of a dark skin employee being direct with a question or a response because of the preference to get straight to the point. It's a cultural thing! These communications are not conveyed whilst shouting or whilst having an intimidating nose to nose conversation or using capital letters in the body of an email, but a polite direct interaction. It seems that the ritual of making small talk before venturing into a *'May I....'* question for example, will be viewed more positively by the recipient than a direct question. (Yes, it's something I learnt on an Assertiveness Course.... or two.......). And please do not use the pathetic excuse of *'But it was the way that you asked'* rubbish as if your sensibilities had been traumatised. You are no Jane Bennet. No shouting occurred and you clearly understood the language spoken but expected one to bow or to go on bended knee when asking the question.

Red Flag: Self-reflection of one's values and behaviours before contrasting them with the organisation's expected rules of one's conduct, is always a worthwhile practice.

Harassment

Organisational policies provide the rules of expected behaviour within the workplace that is free of harassment which is mostly adhered. It may still occur and take on different forms depending on the sex of the perpetrator. Unwanted verbal or physical conduct in the workspace is not what a dark skin employee signed up to when joining the organisation.

A woman scorned takes on a new meaning when the recipient of the unhealthy conduct is another woman. (Get your heads out of the gutter!!). Bringing your talent into the team and displaying competencies that others may not have can become a source of jealousy, often resulting in unwanted conduct that becomes persistent in the attempt to diminish any established credibility or reputation. The misconduct may take various forms from completely ignoring your presence in the office, organising meetings and team events in your absence, to rumour spreading, blindsiding, using your precious personal mug to provoke a reaction, belittling, or taking your ideas for their own, and any other conceivable action to isolate you from other colleagues.

Admittedly, men are equally disturbing with their antics as their deranged female counterparts. But when sex becomes the reason for the unwanted conduct, things may take a sinister turn. Holding a confidential conversation with a male colleague at their desk, either standing or stooping down when no chairs are free for you to sit on, is not an unusual practice in the workplace.

When getting up from a stooped position, do so with great care otherwise you may grab hold of your colleague's leg to steady yourself for which you must apologise. But then do not be surprised to find yourself the subject of possible disciplinary action, because the colleague has decided to raise a complaint of sexual harassment against you. Now had the colleague been

79

Denzel Washington or Brad Pitt then you would wholeheartedly refute the allegation with the hope that the hearing panel allowed you to re-enact the experience. The unfortunate reality in this instance was that the extremely mature colleague had the looks and personality of Gollum, which made the experience even more horrifying.

Supporting in projects provide the basis for meeting and working alongside a variety of people outside the usual team members. It is normal to like some colleagues and work more effectively with them than others. The establishment and maintenance of a good working relationship is not, however, permission to disrupt the relationship dynamics and make sexual advances.

Working alongside a colleague and supporting them so that they perform in their frigging job is the reason for you being hired. Establishing common ground and responding to the colleague's concerns promptly serves a reason, that they will trust the advice provided to enable them to manage their dysfunctional team more effectively. Let me reiterate the point so that there is no misunderstanding. I am doing my job!

This should not be interpreted as my fancying you and will jump into your marital bed because you think I am not like other women. Or that I will schedule quickies in between meetings because you have formed the warped notion that my courteous behaviour or concerns about your wellbeing is a declaration of my love for you. It does not give you permission to flick your hand across my breast telling me that you were brushing away a speck of dust from my jacket when I'm wearing a dress.

It does not give you permission to creep up behind me to whisper compliments in my ear. I do not want to hear that you were thinking of me whilst you were making out with your wife, I do not want to hear your thoughts of how animalistic you believe I must be in the bedroom, outdoors, up a frigging tree. And please, do not make drunken calls or send text messages to my personal number which I had to disclose because the department took forever to provide me with work equipment. I do not engage because I was doing my job and performing sexual favours was not and will never be a part of my job description!

Red Flag: Can't right now, I'm still cussing! Of all the organisations in the world, I had to step into this one!!

Ethnicity

Stop treating ethnicity as a collective grouping of dark-skinned people. Pardon, you do not believe that organisations have this attitude. Watching early morning UK breakfast shows made me wonder if a black skin presenter had ever sat on the hot red sofa. I see white skin people and I see brown skin people, but no black skin people.

Having referenced earlier how organisations attempt to demonstrate inclusivity, I am reminded of a story regaled by a relative about their Black History month workplace event. The event organisers arranged for senior managers to speak with large groups of the diverse workforce on their experiences of being black. The senior manager at the event my relative attended, was a brown skin manager who spoke of a former black skin colleague's experience of racism in a former workplace. Understandably, my relative and fellow black skin colleagues were incensed at this display of disrespect which reflected a perception that all dark skin employees were the same. Not only did the organisation suffer a loss of credibility, it also lost some of its talented employees, including my relative.

Placating a brown skin individual in roles to show representation of '*blackness*' is both insulting and offensive, yet this act has become common practice in organisations which does nothing but demonstrate a prejudice. Africans and South Asians are ethnically different people.

Red Flag: Stop using other ethnicities to represent the voice, the views, and the experiences of black skin people.

Colourism

There is no avoiding the topic of colourism because it is the reason the rhyme existed. The preference of lighter over dark skin colours was acutely reflective within the senior levels of organisational structures where I had worked and where diversity was promoted. This absence of black employee representation at these levels demonstrated that black skin employees continued to be overlooked for promotions and therefore in other parts of the employment cycle.

Employees always hope to be successful when applying for promotions, especially when there is a great possibility of securing the role after demonstrating their competence. When the lack of success is not because of poor interview performance, or the lack of knowledge or experience but that of having a different skin colour, not once, not twice…. What adds insult to the injury of not securing a promotion, is being instructed by your manager to train the newly appointed white or lighter skinned employee to do the frigging job that you were denied.

Red Flag: A walk through the departments, or a glimpse at the organogram on the intranet will evidence whether colourism is an active unwritten rule within the organisation.

Equal Pay

Disproportionate treatment because of the difference of skin colour is also evidenced in the pay arrangements offered to dark skin employees for their talents. Examples include being part of a newly established team of equivalent grades, but the starting pay is at the lowest pay point, unlike those of fellow team members who do not share your skin colour. The yearly performance review where all development and challenging targets are achieved but gains you the basic pay increase, whereas your white skin colleague who met the general duties of their role, is awarded with a higher pay increase.

Challenging equal pay in a newly restructured team where your role is the only one of three that is relocated into a lower pay band, yet your duties continue to be equivalent to your white male colleagues. Or the expressed terms of pay agreed with unions not being honoured because you chose to remain in your new role following a restructure. Conversely, your white skin colleagues of equivalent grades benefit from the pay increase on surrendering their new roles for employment elsewhere.

Pigeoning your middle management job amongst the group list of directors whose salaries increased significantly following the restructure, was no justification to deny the pay increase, which was both unethical and unfair.

Red Flag: Unethical and disproportionate treatment are currently making great media headlines.

Summary

We all belong to humanity, but our ethnicities and nationalities differ. Our life experiences, of family, friends, beliefs, and education influenced by social and economic circumstance, make us who we are which is to be valued. Employment is the opportunity for these differences to blend, to work and learn from each other whilst achieving the organisation's objectives. The psychological and expressed contractual promises made by organisations that their rules will ensure the fair treatment of all employees in all matters whilst operating on their behalf is accepted by employees on the value of trust. A trust, as can be noted above, that is often manipulated and abused by individuals seeking to control and transform difference into sameness.

Sameness in the execution of work duties may stifle initiative and creativity but if it is a requirement of the role, it will be accepted. Sameness in the conduct and adherence to the organisational rule is also accepted when it is consistently applied to all workforce members. Sameness does not, however, give permission to disregard equal treatment and common decency which is the expectation of all those who enter the work environment.

Do you get it? A balanced and inclusive workforce is achievable where mutuality of obligations and respect exists.

CHAPTER 7

Blockade to Employment

My business studies days introduced me to Abraham Maslow's *'Hierarchy of Needs'* which became my motivational template for achieving personal goals, no matter how large or small. From securing employment with a decent wage to building a nest egg to afford the living I wanted. It was not unusual to work long hours where necessary to achieve targets and gain deserved recognition, but the intrinsic benefits of employment were not always a given.

A desire to work within an inclusive environment where mutual respect existed was more a hope than an expectation, but it was noted that joining an organisation did not automatically transform colleagues into friends. Friends already existed outside of the workplace although any gained internally were seen as a positive. Development opportunities to broaden skills and knowledge through training and secondments inspired new career pathways. Organisational rules that were equitably applied provided opportunities towards gaining promotions where skills and achievements demonstrated suitability for the next step up the corporate ladder. There was an expectation, however, that there would be no requirement to kiss ass or rub shoulders with senior representatives of the organisation to gain a promotion because one was not a contortionist and would only go down on bended knee to a Supremely Higher Being and Divine Power.

This is not an unreasonable assertion of the basic wishes of an employee when seeking to join an organisation, yet the first challenge for most, especially dark skin people, are the hurdles placed before them when attempting to access employment. Although recruitment was my least favourite HR activity that would be avoided whenever possible, the current recruitment methods utilised by organisations have left me more than disheartened. The lapse in ethical best practices shown to candidates when organisations recruit to fill their vacancies has in my view, created new employment barriers rather than make the process simpler.

When identifying the existence of institutional and systemic racism in organisations, Lord Macpherson highlighted recruitment as the first of many barriers placed before dark skin candidates to overcome. Understanding the various activities and behaviours that give rise to bias at the early stages of employment bodes well in removing these restrictions, some of which will now be explored.

Step 1: Update your job description before you post a vacancy.

Updating job descriptions and role profiles to add or remove duties so that they align to the needs of the team, department, and the organisation's goals, is not unreasonable and should be reviewed frequently. Be aware though that the longer the job description the more disinteresting the role becomes to potential candidates rather than an exciting new challenge. Likewise, where organisations expect candidates to sell themselves in interviews, candidates expect a reciprocal effort with adverts and job descriptions. The responsibility for such tasks sits with the recruiting manager alongside the HR and Recruitment teams.

Best practice when setting competency requirements, should be maintained and be realistic. For example, qualification requirements for the duties outlined in a job description can often be excessive or restrictive and disregard comparable years of experience. This is not a lowering of the organisation's standards but broadening the scope and talent of the candidate pool. Where in doubt, then reflect upon the previous candidates appointed in the organisation who were considered the best of all candidates, ticking all the right boxes with the outstanding interview performance, only to find them completely incompetent at doing the job.

A well-known UK recruitment business once contacted me to undertake an interim role for a regional service, at a time when equality was high on the agenda. The recruitment consultant had reached out because of my experience and newly achieved Human Resources qualification which was a requirement for the role. They were boastful about their dual role in producing the job description and profile for the post, but my suggestion of lowering the qualification requirement to include an appropriate years' experience as a means of expanding the scope of candidates, went down like a lead balloon. Pointing out the restrictions being placed upon candidates, especially community workers with the relevant years and valuable first-hand experience who may lack the professional qualification, was pointless. It was common sense really, but I spent several days not answering my mobile phone because the consultant just would not accept '*No*' for an answer.

Step 2: How Serious Are You About Building an Inclusive Workforce?

Job vacancies typically express the organisation's commitment to equality, diversity, and inclusion in the last paragraph at the bottom of an advert, or a job description which screams out to all who reads it that inclusion is not a priority. Yet it is one of the first things that potential dark skin candidates want to see from the outset, whether when reading a job description, or on the opening pages of the organisation's website displaying its values.

Step 3. Review Your Internal Talent before Embarking on External Recruitment Exercises.

Where there is a need to acquire specialist skills for a project or to fill a vacancy, it is understandable that the organisation may need to search externally for a candidate. However, before pursuing this route, take the time to review the skills of existing employees because you are likely to find what you need. I have lost count of the number of times I have interviewed for a role only to be told that the successful candidate appointed was an employee. Please do not waste the precious time of candidates in this way. Any reasonable

91

employer will advertise their vacancies internally before pursuing an external search for the right candidate.

Skills assessments of the workforce should be a frequent activity in organisations as there is always hidden talent waiting to be discovered that avoids the significant costs associated with hiring external recruitment consultants or interim contractors. Just by simply having conversations with employees about their work experiences and aspirations, I have been able to persuade managers to place employees into vacant roles which they had previously encountered problems filling. It was disappointing to find that these managers were not aware that the skillset they sought were within reach in their respective departments and yes, they were the talents of dark skin employees. Whilst my approach may have been informal, skills auditing system or meaningful discussions within appraisal review meetings would have saved these managers and their organisations a lot of time and money.

Step 4. Expand Your Network to Reach Diverse Candidates

If you do what you have always done, you will get the same result. I once achieved a diverse workforce through dedicated efforts, not just by posting adverts in the local media and job centres, but by hand delivering posters to local diverse community organisations. Admittedly, this was a couple of decades ago, but I would expect the same approach with media platforms simplifying the process. Restricting the advertising of roles to your organisation's website or through recruitment organisations has its limitations. Organisations that have anti-racist initiatives embedded within their structures may have various managers affiliated to community organisations where the prospect of reaching diverse candidates becomes a much easier task. You can never go wrong with advertising vacancies on local community radio stations and newspapers as there is always a jewel to be found.

Step 5. Avoid Complacent Recruitment Organisations.

How many organisations stipulate an anti-racist requirement in the terms of their agreement with the recruitment organisation sourced to fill vacancies? How many recruitment organisations provide equality data on candidate applications? If the answer to these questions is none, then how do you qualify being an inclusive organisation when access to employment, the primary source preventing dark skin employees from gaining access to the organisation, is not monitored? Organisations conducting its own recruitment activities collate equality data to monitor its effectiveness and to make improvements where necessary. Why then would these steps be disregarded when utilising a recruitment organisation?

Ethical recruitment practices which organisations follow in the search for suitable candidates are not common practice to some recruitment organisations. The lack of courtesy shown to prospective candidates is reflected upon both the organisation and the recruitment service utilised. Candidates will make the effort to complete forms and hold preliminary interviews with the recruitment organisation before being interviewed again with the client organisation. Providing constructive feedback if the candidate is unsuccessful in securing the job is not unreasonable and is preferable to the staple '*the successful candidate had more experience*' comments, so be considerate.

Step 6 - Application Forms

On applying for a senior HR role on an American organisation's website, I began to complete the equality data when prompted then stopped in my tracks because the nature of the questions asked bore no relevance to my ability to do the advertised job. Not only did questions seek information about my secondary school which I had left a couple of decades ago (I'm being polite here!!) but also the highest qualification attained by my parents and free school meals eligibility. It also

94

wanted to know whether I had a relative already employed within the organisation.

Firstly, the role was not positioned within a high security risk level to warrant these types of questions. Neither did the role require my working with the worldwide workforce, but with those within the designated local structure. Requiring candidates to complete a disclosure and barring service check to ensure that they met a specific criterion of suitability for the post, would have been reasonable if the organisation had any concerns about a candidate's suitability.

But questions about secondary school qualifications that have since been superseded with higher or professional qualifications, is non sensical. A curriculum vitae/resume covers the candidate's employment history of a period of 10 years which provides a useful source of information to reflect the candidate's skills and experience. Questions regarding parents' origin, education, or free school meals are all irrelevant and intrusive and not dissimilar to asking how many bathrooms breaks I take each day, which is none of your frigging business!!

Whatever purpose for these questions, for me they were a deterrent. Unless a candidate is offered a job and relevant employment checks are conducted, no such information should be asked for or disclosed. The only occasion where I have ever disclosed my parent's origin was when I joined the Civil Service where it was relevant at that point in time. Outside of these circumstances, such questions can only be viewed as overtly biased aimed to restrict or deselect the employment access of dark skin candidates, whose social and educational experiences may differ significantly to those more privileged candidates.

This issue highlights a problem within recruitment practices where anti-discrimination standards established in the UK contrasts to those practices utilised by global organisations operating within the country. Adopting the host country's recruitment practices would avoid racism and all the other isms that fall under the protection of the UK's Equality Act 2010.

Currently in the UK, equality monitoring questions remains optional for candidates to complete, and the data collected forms part of the analysis undertaken by the organisation to improve equality initiatives. This process is completely independent of the interviewing and selection of candidates. I noticed that on those occasions of refusing to complete the intrusive questions, my job application to the recruiting organisation was not progressed to the next stages. Yes, it could have been for other reasons...

Step 7. Sifting Candidate Applications

The CIPD provides guidance on the recruitment process especially on the sifting of candidate applications. It advocates that anyone involved in the recruitment process should have the necessary up to date training, knowledge, and skill to ensure that the decision-making process is effective and fair. This practice helps to remove bias when recruiting potential employees and highlights an awareness of the *'like me'* bias that often intrudes upon the process. Panel members may be guided by their own personal views and expectations when assessing candidates' profiles, educational affiliations, work experiences and any other traits which become the basis for unfair interview selection.

To avoid this pitfall, the recruiting manager together with interview panel members or HR, if necessary, should conduct this process to constructively debate the interview selection decision. Whilst these steps may not be possible for small business owners who have limited resources, there is no excuse whatsoever for large public and commercial organisations for non-compliance of this recommended practice.

Step 8. The Interview

The importance of training interview panel members also serves as a reminder that the interviewers are representatives of the organisation. The conduct in interviews provides candidates with a first impression of the established culture and standards that lies within.

First impressions are a two-way street for both panel members and candidates, yet it rarely ceases to amaze me the reactions of the interview panel members whenever I enter the interview room or appear on a web call. It is difficult for any individual to hide their surprised or shocked expression, and on rare occasions the look of sheer disgust, instead of having a smiling face welcoming the candidate to the interview. The phrase 'animal in headlights' comes to mind whenever I recall these interviews because the panel members' reactions were not because I exposed my chest or had make-up running down my face. No, it was because they never expected the candidate with the name of Barbara McDonald, to be a black woman.

Even now, with the use of modern media to hold interviews online during the pandemic, I saw those expressions and knew automatically that the role would be offered elsewhere. As well as the convenience of using modern media, there are the challenges with signal problems and the delays with transmission. What is worse, however, is the state of interview panel member's attire or the location of their interviews. If candidates must make the effort to look professional as if attending the interview on site, it would not be unreasonable for panel members to make the reciprocal effort when conducting interviews online. Which leads me to the interviewer who conducted my interview from their boyishly styled bedroom. They were more interested in learning whether I would look after them as well as, or even better than their current HR manager, rather than exploring my experience for the role that I was being interviewed for. All I have to say to you is clean up your bloody mess! No one wants to see your 'toys' on an unmade bed!!

Step 9. Relevant Interview Questions

All interview questions are meant to be meritocracy based, centred on the candidate's ability to perform the tasks set out in the job description. Interview questions must be consistently applied to all candidates and relevant to the vacant position to avoid a difference in treatment. There are many services on social media that provides guidance to candidates on how to sound experienced and knowledgeable when answering interview questions. For me this is the most painful part of the recruitment ritual.

Direct questions are preferable than the dozen time wasting exploratory '*tell me about*' questions that allows bias to creep in because the favourite buzz word of the day was not articulated. I would rather have a constructive conversation about my skills and experience whilst learning more about the requirements of the post instead of wasting time.

When having trouble securing a job, the advice given to me was to '*be more subservient*' to get my foot through the door of the employing organisation. The reason was explained that panel members may feel intimidated by my knowledge and experience although I thought my quirky humour, boredom in some instances or the noticeable grey hair generation x membership, may have been contributing factors. New interviewing approaches that differ from the current stagnant methods are needed desperately. Having seen a few new recruitment software products online that claim to use unbiased selection methods in all its processes, may be the new starting point for this much needed change.

Step 10. Preferred Candidate Appointment

As each candidate is interviewed, panel members will assign a score based on the quality of the candidate's performance to establish the best person for the vacant post. The highest scoring candidate is the most suitable for the role, having demonstrated that their competencies best align to the job description and therefore the needs of the business.... ideally. A shift from the highest scoring candidate to the best candidate who will fit into the team occurs when panel members begin to knit pick and allow bias to creep into the process. To assimilate or not, results in a perceived justification of the highest scored candidate being *'not quite what we were looking for'* and replaced with another candidate deemed *'a better fit'* which makes the entire recruitment process unfair, in my view. Such code speak can be interpreted as the best type of person who will fit into the team and organisation because of the shared *'like me'* traits.

I recall an occasion where a recruitment panel interviewing candidates for three vacant roles in a department had made their appointment decision at great speed. It transpired that the successful candidates were all related to or known to all the recruitment panel members. After requesting copies of the sifting and interview scoring documents to review, I found that none of the highest scoring candidates had been selected for any of the jobs. In fact, two of the highest scoring candidates were dark skin and the recorded reasons for their non selection for the jobs were that they *'Didn't speak English good'*. Suffice to say, none of the preferred candidates were hired and the recruitment drive was rerun with different panel members which avoided any possible risk of discrimination claims against the organisation. It was appropriate to allow the line manager to deal with this act of misconduct.......

Step 11. Starting The Employment Contract.

I recall a time when organisations would offer either a weekly or monthly advance in salary to aid new appointees financially whilst they settled into their new role. This gesture was helpful for any new employee who needed the assistance and helped to establish a dual level of trust and commitment in the employment relationship. Such gestures are no longer apparent and yet such a meaningful benefit would aid many new employees irrespective of whether they have a protective characteristic or not. The alternative solution is to ensure that all newly appointed employees on the starting point of the organisation's lowest pay scale, receives a salary that is no less than the living wage.

Inductions are extremely beneficial to new employees as it provides the opportunity to meet team members and learn more about the organisation's objectives. The best inductions attended were those group sessions where each head of a function conducted a presentation about their responsibilities followed by a question-and-answer session. Other types of inductions were those prearranged meetings with key employees and managers with whom the recruit would mostly interact. Whilst these inductions were beneficial, they all lacked the presence of, or a meeting with a representative from HR, who are responsible for maintaining the cordial relationship of both employees and the employing organisation. Articulating the organisation's standards, expectations and zero tolerance towards discrimination from the outset at induction sessions would go some way towards building the illusive inclusive workforce.

Step 12. Recruitment Organisations (Business & Agency)

Recruitment businesses and agencies are the new recruitment mechanism utilised in modern times to fill vacant posts within organisations. In turn, organisations utilise these services for its cost saving and what can often be a labour-intensive activity. These recruitment organisations are in my view, an additional modern restriction to the access of employment, exacerbated by their creative self-imposed rules which are detrimental to candidates.

The reliance on recruitment organisations, is not always fortuitous for organisations seeking to fill a vacancy, as they are seen by many candidates as modern-day salespeople. Instead of knocking on the door to sell some crap that you have no desire to purchase, recruitment consultants will despatch high levels of emails or telephones calls to unsuspecting candidates about job vacancies. Very few of these ~~sales'~~ recruitment consultants will have taken the time to read a candidate's curriculum vitae which they found through a quick word search on various jobs websites, to determine their suitability for the role. But like a salesperson, the consultant's primary goal is to achieve their targets and to make as much commission in the process. Unless the consultant has a good working relationship with the client organisation, or has informed knowledge about the vacancy, any general questions posed by the candidate are likely to go unanswered.

Role Misfit

The goal of the recruitment consultant is to find a suitable candidate match to slot into the vacancy at the client organisation. The absence of most of the essential skills sought by the client is irrelevant because they have found a numpty that will suffice for the client's consideration. A deciding factor when placing a candidate's details before the client is whether the candidate has had any former work experience in the client's sector. The candidate's reluctance to return to such work environments and their new career aspirations is of no consequence because the consultant has a task to complete to get paid, so the more ~~victims~~ candidates found for the client the better. Effective persuasion otherwise known as manipulation or where desperate, downright begging are the techniques used to influence the candidate to apply then attend the interview, only to discover that the human resources specialist was being interviewed for an accounting position.

Data Protection

Where the candidate is unsuccessful in securing the client's vacant post, there is likely to be no feedback or any further communication from the consultant who has already moved on to their next ~~victim~~ recruitment project. This leaves the candidate oblivious to the management of their personal data, whether it will be stored securely until such time it is destroyed or whether it is sold to all and sundry.

Recruitment consultants will frequently seek the candidate's personal data such as their date of birth and partial or full national insurance number which unbeknown to some candidates, represents their British identity. The reasons for consultants requesting this disclosure will usually be explained away as a client's request or an inability for the recruitment organisation to progress the candidate's application without the disclosure. So, the candidate faces a dilemma, to provide the requested information and hope they are selected for the perfect job at a superb organisation or refuse to disclose and walk away from an opportunity of a lifetime. The latter is preferable to maintain the integrity of personal data than to disclose it to continually revolving recruitment organisations diseased with a consistently high staff turnover. No positive outcomes occurred on the occasion where disclosure was provided, no feedback, no interview, nothing. This serves as a reminder to candidates that there is no legal requirement to provide this type of personal data outside of the parameters of the offer and the acceptance of an employment contract.

Complaints

Once a candidate has been secured in a contract in the client organisation, the recruitment consultant becomes the main contact for the candidate to address any general queries whilst they get settled into the role. However, once problems occur within the client organisation, consultants are less likely to be active in resolving the problems as the client relationship is deemed more valuable than the mistreatment of the candidate.

Intimidation and other misconduct such as the refusal or the delay in authorising time sheets or travel expenses, preventing the candidate from being paid for their hard work, is not uncommon. However, do not be surprised to discover on closer inspection of the contract with the recruitment organisation, that they absolve themselves from all forms of responsibility should the candidate and the client's relationship fall apart.

Unfair Pay

The introduction of the UK Government's IR 35 financial arrangement is the most hated barrier to fair employment opportunities for candidates who are independent contractors and who are not placed on a fixed term contract directly with the client organisation. This mechanism of control assumes that contractors either abuse or avoid tax payments and so they are now required to make such payments through a third-party organisation otherwise known as an umbrella company. These umbrella companies are utilised by recruitment organisations to provide the administration services relating to the candidate's contract and pay arrangements.

The first thing to understand about the unfair treatment is that the rate of pay advertised by the recruitment organisation is not the pay that the candidate will receive for their hard work. The recruitment organisation receives a payment from the client organisation for finding a candidate to fill a vacant post. The contract for service that is issued to the contractor alongside the administration of time sheets and the payment of wages is carried out by the umbrella company.

The contractor is obliged to pay for this Hobson's choice privilege because unbeknown to them, when signing the contract, they became an '*employee*' of the umbrella company and not the recruitment organisation. The cost of this administrative service is deducted from the weekly or monthly pay, but that is not all folks, tax and national insurance deductions are duly accounted for on the issuing of the contractor's payslip. As are the deductions for the employer's tax and the employer's apprenticeship levy which are the employer's costs.

The levy is a payment that employers with more than 250 employees must contribute towards the Government's funding of the national apprenticeship scheme. The contractor is an employee of the umbrella company who is the employer, therefore how are these charges fair?

What Next?

Whether knowingly or unknowingly, organisations through their recruitment outsourcing activities, have created new barriers for all candidates attempting to access all employment opportunities. Once a resource utilised for acquiring specialist and unique skillsets in the jobs marketplace, recruitment organisations are now established gatekeepers providing a Hobson's choice recruitment service.

There will no doubt be some recruitment organisations who provide client organisations with an ethical recruitment service of a high standard. Where this is not the case, then consideration should be given to the return of inhouse recruitment activities. Technological advancements in recruitment software may now enable the process of finding the right candidates for a vacant position, more cost effectively.

Do you get it? Removing recruitment barriers, whether old or new systems and practices, will aid in the objective of achieving inclusivity within the workplace.

CHAPTER 8

Management Styles

The management of employees is an enormous responsibility placed upon the shoulders of individuals that it should never be taken lightly. Managers operating at all levels of the organisation are not only empowered to lead a team of employees to deliver the business objectives but are also empowered to execute the terms within the contracts of those employees.

From hiring and developing new employees, to ensuring tasks are conducted appropriately. Monitoring, and appraising to mentoring and coaching to engage employee commitment. Delivering results utilising the skills and the strengths of team members to initiating formal disciplinary or performance improvement action where misconduct or under performance occurs. For employees, the effectiveness of managers is determined not just by the results delivered for the organisation, but also in the treatment they receive.

Whilst a business studies student, I learnt of two key problems affecting organisations that I had hoped to never experience as a manager. The first was the lack of competency and the inability to manage people. The other was defined as the

'*Peter Principle*', promoting a person to a level of incompetence. Fortunately, organisations offered ways in which these problems could be overcome.

A traditional approach for employees wishing to secure a management position within public organisations, required employees to undergo relevant line management training before securing a temporary secondment into a line management position. This enabled prospective managers to gain practical experience in managing employees, where the assigned line managers of those seconded, would evaluate the performance and make recommendations of further development needs where necessary.

The seconded employee was expected to achieve any proposed further development before any serious consideration was given to their appointment into a management position. Understanding the responsibilities of management through the development of competencies whilst building interpersonal skills, secured a desired promotion to a well-earned status.

Then a new trend emerged where individuals who had no line management experience nor specialist skills were being placed into managerial positions. Committed employees with years of experience who had added value to the organisation and were on route to the next level in their career path were suddenly discarded for a dynamic graduate with a degree. The type of degree did not seem to matter because for decision makers, it confirmed a higher education and provided a great ego boost to the numpty who placed the botany graduate into a senior technical engineering position.

Such escalation into positions of power became achievable through elitist graduate, network, and mentoring schemes. Knowing the right person to cajole, sweet talk and to brown nose incisively became the new trend. Competency flew out of the top floors of office buildings and nose-dived into the pavement below in disbelief whilst kiss ass fluttered through the glass ceiling to claim its power.

Who you knew, not what you knew became a corporate priority as these new entrants were viewed to inject new life into outdated practices. All at the expense of existing employees whose upskilling and broadening of knowledge throughout the years were replaced with favouritism. For dark skin employees, it was just another playground hurdle of the '*like me*' disease to overcome.

There are many academic books that critique management styles and behaviours in organisations which is enlightening.

112

From my personal experience, I have consistently found four types of managers throughout my career and whatever the sector, their conduct has remained the same. These management types are:

The Narcissistic Manager

The typical management style of this individual responsible for overseeing a team of people or function is remote. That is to say that they are absent from any activities going on in the department. Participation will occur only in relation to their own specialism if they have one, otherwise the delegation of their responsibilities to subordinates is to be expected. They resume control only when executive members or other senior leaders require their attention.

It is important for the individual to be respected by their peers and so the credit for the hard work and the initiatives of subordinates are taken for their own. They are after all leading the team or department and so any employee working within must know that it is the individual alone and not them who must own the credit for the work, especially if it contributes towards a business success. There will be no dissent from team members who may complain loudly to each other, but they know only too well, the power that the individual holds and the ease at which it will be abused to suppress any objections.

Any restructures or reorganisation taking place will guarantee that the individual retains or promotes themselves into another senior role because of their manipulative influence over decision makers. Decisions over the employees whom they will work alongside are carefully managed as they must only have those loyal subjects who will collude when instructed or are easily controlled, so that they may continue to benefit from any ill-gotten gains. Empire maintained, any threats to destabilise it whether through an employee's inquisitiveness or display of competence must be eliminated. Any formal process such as redundancy, redeployment or any other means that does not expose the individual, will be utilised.

Where these individuals have a specialist skill, it is usually not in the function for which they are held accountable and so procrastination over important decisions is not uncommon. This often exposes the organisation to financial risks, but any such outcome will be attributed to a subordinate's incompetence and not theirs. The status of seniority is controlled through bullying, manipulation, and threats to subordinates, who are reminded

114

through the loss of another ~~victim~~ colleague, that their job security is at risk with any challenge levied at the individual.

Indirect antics using their minions to sabotage credibility are their game of choice, although direct participation is unavoidable because their ego craves recognition. Any tactic is utilised to create hostility and influence the departure of the unwanted.

Externally, that is anywhere outside of the team under its control, this individual may be viewed as a competent leader with a well-established network of professionals. Those peers who are aware and have a preference not to act against the toxic empire built, will themselves have created similar structures with the individual's arm's length support.

For team members, they are just amazed that the individual has gotten away with the ~~bunny boiler~~ unprofessional conduct for a great length of time. Yet none have the courage to raise a challenge because their personal needs whether family matters or their pending retirement, forces them to commit to the job until the opportunity arises for them to escape.

The Competent Manager

This manager encompasses the good qualities and expectations outlined in academic books on management capability and effective leadership. They abide by the rule of developing all team members to take over their duties should they suddenly leave, so that the function and the organisation's goals are maintained seamlessly. These individuals have the specialist experience but where this may be lacking, they will be proactive to upskill and to obtain a thorough understanding in their area of responsibility so that they are an effective leader. They utilise all resources to encourage the development within the team, continuously providing team members with opportunities to challenge themselves and to learn new skills to keep abreast of the times.

Credit and praise are given naturally and frequently to employees which boosts moral and the team's performance which is consistently high. Consequently, the individual is valued and respected by all team members and senior leaders. Not open to manipulation, this individual will provide constructive support and critiques to encourage improvements and will be active to resolve any conflict in the team, ensuring that harmony is always maintained, and disciplinary action is taken as an absolute last resort. Having a respect for individuality, all employees receive fair treatment with this manager.

116

The Incompetent Manager (Muppet)

This type of manager is the one that has been promoted to the level of incompetence, either through various organisational schemes or redeployment after being placed at risk of redundancy. Inexperienced in people management and the specialist skills required for the acquired team or department function, these individuals have a steep mountain of learning to climb but may be book smart.

These individuals will often have inflated egos and naively believe in a literal authoritarian style of management when instructing team members, which exposes their incompetence. Strong characters within the team will take advantage of this weakness to manipulate and assume indirect control of the individual and other team members with gestures of a helping hand of support. This seems logical given that the individual does not have a clue about the function for which they are now responsible.

The muppet may have connections through the senior manager who mentored or influenced their appointment into the role and so an affiliation of all things good and bad, binds them. The longer in post, the muppet must learn the meaning of true 'leadership' and begins to transform either into the competent manager or into the narcissist that sets about building their empire. They must also protect themselves from the daggers aimed at their back from the little helpers vying for their position. Either way, the muppet will unfortunately retain their title of incompetence until such time a path is chosen or before their shamefaced mentor throws them under a bus.

The Exhausted Manager

This individual was once competent in their management role, but the constant changing nature of work, increasing workloads, reforms and restructures have made the job burdensome. The lack of constructive support from those in more senior positions or in specialist roles within the organisation has left this individual depleted and beaten down. Whether it is their line manager's refusal to follow through on requests or HR who constantly informs them that *'It's the manager's responsibility'*, there is no constructive support when requested.

The lack of problem solving has resulted in team members ruling the roost where reasonable management instructions are laughed at or carried out under protest. So, the delegation of duties becomes an overload of tasks to complete which is carried out ~~in a zombie mode~~ on autopilot in the hope that local targets are achieved.

A toxic culture reigns within the team or department where organisational expectations are displaced by abusive language and other acts of gross misconduct. All stakeholders are prospective victims and must be blamed for everything in this game of toilet thrones. Reputational damage is measured by the team member at the top of the team's league table holding the record for the most destructive stakeholder impact. Survival for the individual leading this team is founded on the hope to one day escape the abyss they have found themselves in.

Final Thought

These are my observations of the types of managers operating in organisations and are based purely on my experience. What is of interest, however, is how these managers utilise their delegated powers of authority and control and its impact towards any anti-racism strategies that may exist within organisations.

Of all the managers identified above, the competent manager is the only one who would be proactive in maintaining and embedding any equality initiative to achieve a diverse and inclusive team or department. Given the self-serving traits of two of the management types, priority would be to retain the norm and avoid any difference, where possible. The exhausted manager is possibly the more serious offender of inclusion with the toxic team culture impacting upon all stakeholder groups. Employee domination in a department means the informality of its culture becomes a petri dish of bias that contaminates and rejects difference.

Do you get it? The removal of the rose-tinted glasses that blinds organisations to the internal reality of management behaviours, is crucial for equality, diversity, and inclusion to be successful.

CHAPTER 9

The Effectiveness of Human Resources

The previous chapter provided a brief insight into the behaviour of managers when overseeing a team or department of employees. This responsibility is not an easy undertaking and is full of complexities and challenges when attempting to maintain a decent employer and employee relationship. Managers must contend with the different personalities, abilities and individual needs whilst making decisions to drive business objectives.

To support both parties in maintaining the harmonious and effective bond, are those employees who rest within the Human Resources team now known to some as the people service. The strategic and operational activities of HR impacts upon all business functions in an organisation. One key area is employee relations which focuses on regulating the employment relationship by ensuring that employees work cohesively to achieve the organisation's objectives. Organisational policies that align to UK legislation provides a solid foundation for the contractual arrangements between the parties, with equality as its golden nugget which ensures all employees receive fair treatment.

Yet this group of people champions get a negative wrap, having fought for years to be sat at the high table with senior leaders, after undergoing a transition from administrative to meaningful operational and strategic people activists. Where accountability for new initiatives such as equal opportunities was placed at their desks, push back was achieved with the arrival of managing diversity with the onus placed upon individuals. Hiring specialists to manage the promotion of anti-discriminatory strategies within the organisation did not absolve the people champions of their ethical duty of embedding fair and equal treatment within the organisation. The roles differed with one party creating approaches for an inclusive organisation, whilst the other ensured these initiatives were embedded and took appropriate formal action where resistance to anti-discrimination conduct occurred.

So, what went wrong? The constant media reports regarding the mistreatment or disproportionate treatment of dark skin employees or service users are evidence of a significant failure in the anti-discrimination movement. A movement that is central to the HR purpose. It leads me question the point of sitting at the high table if not to mitigate the disadvantages caused to all stakeholders?

My formal studies in human resources occurred some years ago now but it ensured that students had a fundamental understanding of the moral and ethical standards as well as the laws governing the various areas of employment, within the first year of learning. A selection of options enabled students to specialise in a particular field, whether in recruitment, employee relations, organisational development, pay and benefits or ~~training~~ learning and development to gain the Chartered Institute of Personnel and Development (CIPD) accreditation. Over the years the syllabus has altered with the changing nature of this specialism, but the foundations of expected standards remain intact.

Employee relations and equality were my passion and transferring this knowledge into the workplace became somewhat easier with experience, although different employee personalities and pedantic trade union representatives sometimes made the resolution of straight forward issues somewhat challenging. Having a former career investigating and resolving complaints combined with line management experience made this new career direction a logical next step when the opportunity arose. I knew from the outset that my approach would differ to those personnel or HR managers I had known in the past and who in my opinion, ~~were crap~~ had failed to do the right thing when dealing with my workplace challenges.

Committed to following the recommended best HR practices, the use of case laws, logic, and experience to aid the effective resolution to cases were my means to championing HR practices. I found that it provided employees with the assurance of being heard when their concerns were acted upon. Being proactive and pragmatic provided managers with improved knowledge and confidence to manage teams effectively thereby becoming less reliant upon HR to deal with petty issues.

Any uncooperative employees, namely managers, were politely informed of why their demands could not be supported and provided general details of caselaw where applicable, to support decisions. Occasionally, they would be thrown the book of rules to find an alternate solution to what they commanded, that did not breach the contract or create a financial risk to the employer. Best practice methods when dealing with conflict issues were effective because it promoted fair treatment and an inclusive environment where any lost trust and confidence in managers were restored.

Working in a variety of organisations enabled some new skills development and the updating of others, but practical experience of many HR processes was already known to me, as were equality initiatives. There were many HR professionals who I worked alongside who were as passionate about fair treatment and building an inclusive workplace for all employees, but they at the time did not hold the senior roles within their organisations. Those in position of authority tended to be characters who were either yeah sayers having been in post within the organisation forever, or they were interim contractors.

One organisation comes to mind that had a high level of low paid and vulnerable employee turnover because of unreasonable and uncompromising management expectations. I recall informing a colleague that everything possible would be done to save a vulnerable employee with an exemplary employment record, from being dismissed for a minor misconduct. Days later I was informed that my due to end contract would not be renewed. Clearly, my HR approach did not fit into the culture of this organisation where managers were expected to have their wishes granted. It also seemed too much of a coincidence that mine and another dark skin contractor were the only people out of at least a dozen working within the department, who did not

125

have their contracts renewed. This change allowed for the dominant skin colour group within the department to be fully restored.

Appointing the most appropriate HR professionals to positions of seniority with accountability for the workforce is imperative because fair treatment permeates every area of the HR function. Equality, diversity, and inclusion as a strategic aim of the organisation would be measurable by the tangible improvements evidenced for example, in meaningful and unmanipulated HR staffing data. Yet delving beyond the figures to investigate and remedy the lack of representation and progression of dark skin employees is not always prioritised or given the same attention as say, the downturn in sales figures or the failure of a new product launch. Hence, the illusion that surrounds equality, diversity, and inclusion.

The nature of my work led to my diverse group of friends and associates reaching out to me for assistance whenever they experienced workplace difficulties that posed a challenge to resolve. The more support I provided, the clearer it became that the majority of those aided were dark skin employees. I found it curious that those who were white skin employees would be compensated and their complaints resolved, unlike dark skin employees whose complaints were, I can only politely describe as mismanaged.

This realisation led me to question over the years why, whether from personal experience or when dealing with other people's problems, were these acts being ignored or marginalised when placed at HR's door. My views that white skin people did not understand racism was evidenced when learning that all the participants involved in the cases, line managers, HR, the chairpersons, and representatives were all white skin employees. It appeared that unless overt racist acts of blatant and derogatory name calling were evident, white skin employees did not understand racism in the workplace and so did not deal with these complaints appropriately.

Difficult as it was to reach this conclusion, it explained the lack of constructive action taken to resolve matters. Put your hands up in the air if you have experienced sexual harassment in the workplace? Men too!! The formal process for dealing with the allegation of sex discrimination is not so dissimilar to that of race discrimination, which makes the conduct of my peers in the management of these cases, difficult to believe.

Then, in 2021, the CIPD reported data from the Annual population survey on the UK's HR workforce. It showed that

88% were white skin employees and 12% dark skin and other minority groups. These statistics seemed to support my views which were further verified by another CIPD report showing that HR professionals felt that external support and guidance on dealing with racism in the workplace was lacking.

The UK's Equality and Human Rights Commission (EHRC) was established to police if you will, the equality laws. They provide all the necessary support and guidance to employers, employees, and citizens, to the point of taking enforcement or legal action against law breakers where necessary to ensure the compliance of legal expectations. In a similar manner, the Advisory, Conciliation and Arbitration Service (ACAS) provide resources and proactive services of mediation and dispute resolution prior to workplace cases being presented to an employment tribunal. Or they used to. It was only though my dealings with some recent casework did I learn the extent of the diminished services offered by these and other public organisations. The iron clasp of high ethical and quality standards that once provided a shield of protection within our society had eroded significantly. Replaced instead by a cold blue cloak of draconian control, denying all citizens anything beyond

128

the absolute basics of service. I had no choice but to agree with my peers who had contributed to the surveys.

That said, there is no excuse for ignoring CIPD's standards and recommended best practices when ensuring procedural fairness and natural justice is carried out undiluted within the workplace. Fundamental case laws are always a good source when considering the level of seriousness of a race discrimination allegation. The case of Vento v Chief Constable of West Yorkshire Police (2002) established the three-tier compensation level awarded in race discrimination claims and provides examples of racist acts and behaviours. Reading more recent case laws provided either through a subscribed employment service or any employment law book author provides additional sources of information. Public bodies mentioned above will provide general information and where cases appear to be more complex, then guidance from an experienced employment lawyer who specialises in discrimination law should be sought.

When supporting others with their workplace complaints, there were two reoccurring themes about the service provided by HR that were a cause for concern. The first was the belief held that HR only provided support to managers and not to employees. This belief highlighted the second concern of impartiality, given that HR only provided the outcomes sought by managers. The organisation's complaint process was either mismanaged or manipulated to satisfy a personal wish rather than achieve a just solution. Such actions could only be viewed as serious miscarriages of justice and a significant breach of the employment contracts.

It serves as a reminder that less favourable treatment shown towards a dark skin employee in the course of their employment, is treated as being done by the organisation. Whether the discriminatory actions or behaviours are carried out with or without the approval or knowledge of other employees is irrelevant because the organisation is still held liable. A liability that HR is expected to prevent rather than enable because any claims of ignorance, incompetence, or the mismanagement of a given situation, is not an accepted defence for discrimination.

Do you get it? The failure to maintain the fundamental ethical standards of fairness in all HR practices, has significantly eroded the trust and confidence that dark skin employees once had in organisations.

CHAPTER 10

~~Hobson's~~ HR's Choice

'*Hobson's Choice*' by Harold Brighthouse is another of my favourite books read in secondary school and the old 1954 black and white film featuring the brilliant British actors Sir John Mills and Sir Charles Laughton, is a must watch. Throughout my career I found myself frequently making the statement, '*Well, it's a Hobson's Choice, isn't it?*' when either placed in or asked to deal with a difficult situation. For me, '*Hobson's Choice*' meant having no real choice at all, of being placed between that rock and a hard place with barely an option at my disposal. Leaving me to go with flow and to hope to high heaven that I was able to reach the other side of the crap that I had been handed. But that was the whole point, of having a free choice where only one thing was offered, '*Do it or else!*'.

A HR consultant's online complaint about line managers allowing problems amongst team members to escalate before seeking HR intervention had me intrigued. There may have been many reasons for the manager's perceived complacency, but it prompted me to question whether timely and pragmatic support had previously been provided to resolve the issues. Was HR doing what they had always traditionally done hence the problem escalation instead of using their initiative to achieve a different and timely outcome? Being inflexible and avoiding collaborative problem-solving options whilst attributing blame elsewhere with the standard repetitive responses of '*It's the line manager's responsibility*' is such a cop out and one of my pet hates when working in HR departments. Whether it is a manager seeking support, a sarcastic remark from an employee, or a noticeable change in monthly workforce data, whatever the indicator the onus remains with HR to take the appropriate action to resolve the issue with the manager.

Reflecting specifically upon those race discrimination casework dealt with, I discovered trends that highlighted a failure on the part of organisations and specifically HR, to pursue a due process when dealing with complaints. I found myself asking a series of questions when attempting to resolve these issues which I now share with the hope that they may serve as guidance when dealing with such cases.

1. Have you understood the nature of race discrimination presented?

2. Have you provided constructive support to the employee?

3. Have you checked that the formal process has not been abused or mismanaged?

4. Have you protected the employee from being caused any further detriment?

5. Have you trivialised the allegation?

6. Have you reinterpreted the allegation?

7. Have you influenced the process of a race discrimination complaint?

8. Have you ignored the collusion of other parties towards the complainant?

The following information are practical examples of how HR, the moral compass of organisations, have chosen to utilise their influence to conceal the detriment caused to dark skin employees in the workplace. Manipulating the outcomes of complaints of racism can only be viewed as asserting control over the employees to either prevent or restrict their voices when seeking justice. The Hobson's choice that was offered in all these instances was for the complainant to accept their given situation, which HR appeared to view as normal. Whether knowingly or unknowingly, HR who are employees of the organisation, were enabling racial discrimination of dark skin employees in the workplace. Now let us look at these questions in a little more detail so that lessons may be learnt.

1.   Have you understood the nature of race discrimination presented?

When an employee raises a complaint of race discrimination, the first step is reading through the complaint to try and identify where the act of discrimination has occurred, then possibly to refresh your memory of the law by reading the organisation's policy. In those situations where it has been a while since dealing with a case, I always reach for an employment law book to refresh my memory in more detail before reading where necessary any relevant and recent employment tribunal case rulings.

On being asked to provide support to an appeal panel, I was presented with the papers of the former hearing and informed by the HRBP that the complaint bore no relevance to race discrimination. They felt the employee had used the formal process to moan about their colleagues following a breakdown in the working relationship, and so the employee's complaint had not been upheld.

The nature of race discrimination was clearly articulated and evidenced on reading the casefile and yet neither the HRBP nor the Employee Relations specialist who had provided guidance on the earlier hearing had failed to properly consider the complaint. Instead of remaining objective and focusing on the collated facts of the mistreatment and the law, the hearing had steered towards the subjective statements of witnesses. As a result of the panel reaching the decision that the broken relationship could be restored, the employee's complaint was not upheld. It was difficult not to note the that alleged perpetrators of the mistreatment and the employee who had raised the complaint, shared the same dark skin colour.

The organisation's policy clearly stated the definition of race discrimination being an issue of skin colour.... or ethnicity, or ethnic origin or nationality, which was not indecipherable. In this instance, the employee was one ethnic origin, and the alleged perpetrators were another. The serious acts of mistreatment which included the denial of benefits provided to all employees, were aimed to orchestrate the employee's removal from the team because of their ethnic difference. The white skin hearing panel members and the HR specialists may have perceived race discrimination as a black and white skin problem which led to them to seeing only sameness in this case. Their recommendation could only be viewed as offensive, given

135

that the detriment caused to the employee had been completely ignored which meant that the misconduct of the perpetrators was deemed acceptable behaviour by these senior representatives of the organisation. The employee who had clearly stated the belief that the less favourable treatment was because of their ethnicity, had been let down by all those expected to ensure a fair solution to the complaint. This meant that any attempts to mitigate the previously misjudged hearing outcome was lost.

2. <u>Have you provided constructive support to the employee?</u>

Raising a grievance or being the subject of disciplinary action is a heavy emotional burden for any employee to carry. Access to the Employee Assistance Programme (EAP), if one is contracted to the organisation, is a useful support to employees as are trade unions or employee representatives who are an additional means of providing guidance. However, not all organisations offer this impartial and independent support to their employees. Where those occupying senior positions in the organisation may receive support from an impartial manager internally, those employees in lower pay bands are not always shown the same courtesy, especially where complaints are raised against their managers.

In such circumstances, consistency with the support systems provided to all employees is important.

3. Have you checked that the formal process has not been abused or mismanaged?

The ACAS Code of Disciplinary and Grievance procedure provides the foundation of good practice for the organisation's rules on natural justice and procedural fairness. Ensuring that the process is followed correctly is the responsibility of HR who ensures that its integrity is not compromised. Letters issued to the employee, confirmation of interview and hearing dates, named chairperson, provision of hearing packs are examples of some of the many tasks that HR will carry out to ensure the employee is fully informed and supported throughout the process.

Unfortunately, this is not quite the reality even though HR are in the driving seat of this process of fairness. Suspending a dark skin employee from work and placing them under investigation because of the misconduct carried out by their white skin colleague, is not reasonable. Even when evidence is presented to show that the dark skin employee was not party to or in the location at the time of the alleged misconduct. Or a dark skin employee with a meticulous employment record being disciplined and receiving a final notice for the dereliction of duty because they had an extended lunch break after completing their labour-intensive tasks for the day, alone. Yet none of their white skin colleague, whom they had to wake up mid-afternoon by banging down their front doors after they had failed to attend work that morning, go undisciplined. Or when a dark skin employee appeals the unfair decision of a disciplinary panel and irrespective of the numerous update requests made, their communications are ignored for more than three months. Surely HR knows that evasive responses infer discrimination at play?

Inviting a dark skin employee into a meeting room after their lunch break only for them to find themselves in a formal hearing and being asked to provide their witness account to an incident they learnt about through a third party. Or inviting a disabled dark skin employee into an informal meeting and refusing their request to be accompanied when the manager's tone in the meeting changes into threats of formal action and dismissal. Or denying a disabled dark skin employee the inexpensive reasonable adjustment equipment recommended by specialists some twelve months previous, that would enable their continued employment in an organisation with affiliations to other disability organisations.

The coat tailing of another organisational process to attack, to threaten or to discipline a dark skin employee such as the use of a customer's complaint to build gross misconduct allegations against a dark skin employee. The unsubstantiated *'aggressive behaviour'* allegation on top, exposes the racism at play.

4. Have you protected the employee from any further detriment?

When you receive an employee's complaint of race discrimination against a manager, do you continue to allow the parties to work together or separate the parties until the complaint process is resolved? Relocating either party to another department whilst the allegation is investigated is not unreasonable. To maintain the status quo only enables problems to escalate and subject the complainant to possible further detriment of targeted acts or behaviours causing or exacerbating wellbeing concerns.

When in doubt about what action to take one need only to ask that if the case related to sexual harassment, would you expect the victim and the alleged perpetrator to continue working together? Then why would you not treat the victim of racism in the same manner, given that their dignity and self-respect has also been violated? Yes, we can be pedantic and argue that it all depends on the nature of the discriminatory act, but I would argue otherwise, in that it depends upon the impact of the acts upon the victim.

5. Have you trivialised the allegation?

Race discrimination allegations tend to be trivialised to avoid following the formal process of collating the evidence to support or counter the allegation. A manager raising a grievance against a team member may appear inappropriate when the disciplinary process is available, but the alleged victim sanctioning the alleged perpetrator using the disciplinary process would not make for a just solution.

A manager raising a complaint of race discrimination tend to have their complaint explained away with remarks of them being oversensitive or any other reason that provokes an emotion for the manager to second guess their actions. Irrespective of how complex the circumstances may be, it is the role of HR to remain impartial and ensure that procedural fairness is enacted so that an appropriate resolution is achieved.

6. Have you reinterpreted the allegation?

On receipt of a complaint of race discrimination, did you form a different opinion and decide to guide the investigation towards your personal views rather than establishing and clarifying the

140

facts, as seen in the first example. The simplest questions are rarely asked in these situations, such as '*Why do you believe A's actions or behaviour amount to race discrimination?*' Asking this question shows an acknowledgement of the concern and once the response is presented, HR's role is to ensure that that facts and the context surrounding the actions or behaviours of those involved are impartially investigated. This is after all, the process of fairness.

Speculating and making assumptions to fit personal perceptions of the allegation are yours to own. We all speculate, but these views are not those of the complainant which makes them irrelevant. Their experience of the conduct and its effects on them personally must remain the focus and where assumptions impede or influence the route of the formal process then the complaint has not been taken seriously. This will further add to the stress and burden upon the complainant and may be damaging to the organisation should the matter be escalated to an employment tribunal setting.

7. Have you influenced the process of a race discrimination complaint?

HR are often guilty of attempting to deter complainants from pursuing a race discrimination complaint. One case involved HR

141

pressuring the complainant with unhelpful comments about pursuing the complaint, explaining that it would be *'extremely stressful'* and *'I wouldn't do it if I were you'*. Such manipulation instead of meaningful support is not the behaviour employees expect from HR.

At the start of an interim contract, I learnt of the custom of providing the department leaders with copies of investigation reports so that they could be rewritten to influence the outcome of formal processes. An iron gate was immediately erected and all enquirers chasing a copy of reports were redirected to receive an ass kicking so that the process remained unbiased. Why HR had enabled this practice is unknown, but it was noted that those under investigation were predominantly dark skin employees.

8. <u>Have you ignored the collusion of other parties towards the complainant?</u>

There are occasions where the alleged perpetrator and their associates, whether fellow employees or managers will attempt to either manipulate or influence the outcome of a complaint. In another of my cases, a selected group of witnesses decided to collude when conveying the facts to support the allegation of race discrimination. The collation of evidence meant reviewing other sources of information which exposed their antics, forcing the witnesses to confirm that their actions had been at the behest of the complainant. When this was brought to the complainant's attention, their complaint was promptly rescinded. Unfortunately, the falsely accused and respected alleged perpetrator found their happiness in a new work environment following this outcome, to the disappointment of the organisation.

Collusion may take many forms in the organisation, whether during the formal process as shown above or in general activities for example where an employee is ostracised by team members, which is segregation and unlawful. The employment contract requires employees to work collaboratively within a safe and secure work environment and so nipping these types of toxic behaviours in the butt promptly maintains a workplace where everyone is valued.

Final Comments

The above information provides some examples of the repetitive issues encountered whilst dealing with race discrimination casework and where HR had not performed to an expected standard. Any employee raising a grievance of race discrimination will have done so as a last resort. They will have reflected and reasoned to find alternative explanations for the unfair treatment they have received before reaching their decision to act. It is a destabilising and often a traumatic solo journey for any employee to walk especially where great harm has been caused. Ignoring due process and failing to provide constructive support is undeserving of those who are being brave in their pursuit for natural justice.

Upholding the organisation's duty of care, trust and confidence and processes of fairness are imperative, as they are only a fraction of the employment contract to which dark skin employees agreed to when joining an organisation. The execution of these standards and rules that are applicable to all employees, is not a privilege afforded to HR, it is a moral duty. Any less favourable treatment in the policing of the employment relationship will impact upon the credibility of the organisations' commitments to valuing equality, diversity, and inclusion.

Do you get it? The function of HR service provision must be fit for purpose to provide constructive support to all employees. Rebalancing the workplace scales is required to achieve inclusivity.

CHAPTER 11

Zero Tolerance

As we approach the end of the book of my work life journey in its current guise, I cannot help but reflect on my beginnings of learning to follow rules, where firm punishment was the outcome of any form of disrespect. My parents' simple rules of doing what you were told or to be punished, is not uncommon in many households although the method of punishment may have changed somewhat. '*If you can't hear, you must feel.*'

This same rule is embedded within organisational policies and procedures where employees are expected to comply with the rules or have their contracts of employment terminated. Zero tolerance, unfortunately, appears to have lost its significance in the workplace and has now been diluted with a final chance route for perpetrators to continue their covert acts.

Consider if you will, the police services who have traditionally adopted an overzealous and unjust stance towards dark skin people, stating zero tolerance as its justification. When comparing their handling of terrorist incidents, dark skin perpetrators are shot dead whilst those who are white skin are given bottled water and medical attention after slaughtering innocent people. It is when senior police officials announce to the waiting world media that the white skin perpetrator has mental health issues that we all know that the defence for the terrorist's continued joy to life has just been established.

Zero tolerance was once that mighty axe intended to cut away the infected branches of discrimination to achieve inclusion within society, but it seems now to be a selective method of choice dependent upon the alleged perpetrator's skin colour. It is now time to reclaim the golden axe for its justly intended purpose. The London Metropolitan Police Commissioner is taking such concerted action of enforcing a zero-tolerance stance within the service with the aim of returning the service to its purpose and rebuilding public trust. This is an ambitious endeavour given its bad reputation, but it is the only option for its continued existence, as under any other guise the lack of public trust would remain. I cannot help but to repeat myself in saying that leaders of public and commercial organisations would bode well to follow suit, given the depth and breadth of the toxic behaviours within organisations that continue to be exposed daily. These bad behaviours are not restricted to dark skin people or employees but to all people who have a protected characteristic.

146

The time is now to regain control over workplace injustices with the enforcement of zero tolerance. Zero tolerance expressed in all employment and service contracts, if not already in place would support the drive towards inclusion. Combined with the organisation's policy for procedural fairness, abusers of the rules will be left in no doubt of the consequences of their actions, when organisations follow through on the policy.

As for the consideration of any mitigation in these acts of discrimination, there is none. Not even the excuse of unconscious bias can save a person because we are all adults and are conscious of our biases, so unless the perpetrator is a toddler copying their parents, there is no excuse. Absolutely none! Otherwise, I know of numerous baby bosses in the making that may be a great fit within your organisation. Although the occasional nappy change will be a necessity, this would not be unfamiliar territory for those sat at the high table and operating within toxic environments.

Do you get it? There can no longer be an excuse for discrimination of any form in the workplace.

PART 2

'You Must Feel...'

'Emancipate yourself from mental slavery, none but ourselves can free our minds'. Redemption Song Lyrics by Bob Marley

Many people live a normal life without hindrance, yes there are hurdles to overcome in everyday situations but for others they are compounded by nature's gift of having a different skin colour. The additional barriers that deny a person from being treated like others can take a negative hold of one's confidence. *'You're not good enough...... not intelligent enough...... you must do it this.... you must do that........ do as you are told......... you just do not fit.....'*. The constant bashing at a person's confidence all because of a difference is not an easy thing to live with daily and so to step into an organisation where you must not only conform to the organisation's unspoken rules but receive comparable treatment to the external control systems, becomes another continuous battle.

I realised from an early age that I was not the cause of racist behaviours but that it was the perpetrators who had the problem. The sweating nun hurting me whilst trying the scrub *'the dirt'* from my skin as if to turn me into a white skin person. This was no act of compassion. The teacher who would glare whilst telling me that *'Empty vessels make the most noise'*. Whether I was responding to a friend's request for the use of a pen, or any opportunity they felt that I needed to be told that I was useless. You opened my eyes to the new methods of hate. The teacher who ignored me for two years in one of my favourite subjects that catered to a handful of pupils. Ignoring my hand in the air served a purpose. I had nicely toned arms on leaving school, so thank you.

There were great teachers who encouraged me in subjects that I both loved like art and English, and hated like chemistry, which is what great teacher do, they encourage and inspire. Yet there were the selected few, whose constant attacks of insults to demean, or to humiliate me in front of classmates, or to simply ignore in lessons, was not the education I expected. It became a norm and with it, a realisation of the changing nature of bias towards my skin colour.

The overt distain towards my skin colour was evident but the language used to express the distain differed. There was no racist name calling involved, but I was expected to accept the difference in the treatment received. I had no choice. The

149

preconditioned views that these teachers held associated with my skin colour, denied me the right to be me and to have a voice and a better educational experience.

Wondering whether I would have been treated differently if I had shared the same skin colour as the dominant pupil group in my school, is irrelevant. No child deserves such hostile treatment. Thankfully, there were great teachers and school friends who did not see my skin colour.

Similar racist behaviours were present within the work environment, which held the expectation of my conforming to a singular way of being and to accept the less favourable treatment. But I am my mother's child and like her, I abhor any form of injustice and will stand up for myself and other vulnerable people. Like many other dark skin employees, I endured the negative put downs, the elusive jobs or promotions, the behaviours aimed to disrupt and destabilise my job security and more.

What these individuals did not know was that their negative actions or behaviours was not unknown to me and their attempts to weaken me only made me stronger and even more determined. The Sounds of Blackness encouraged me to remain 'Optimistic' especially through the most challenging of times, singing '*you can win, as long as you keep your head to the sky*' became my mantra. I was motivated to prove only to myself and no other, that I could achieve whatever I wanted to achieve and that I needed no approval from any other person than myself, which made my soul happy. Emancipating myself from other people's stereotypical expectations, was liberating because I was not the character that they perceived me to be. My skin colour made me different, but it was not the only attribute that defined me. My school friendships showed me the uniqueness that each person possesses, is just like a valuable gemstone. Each having different colours, shapes, sizes, characters, composites, and flaws that made them individually beautiful. All preciously gifted and all having great value and purpose.

CHAPTER 12

Human Nature

I cannot deny that there have been some instances where the less favourable treatment shown towards me went unchallenged. It was easier to walk away and to keep the peace amongst team members than to react to a perpetrator's actions or behaviour. I did not consider my inactions to be a sign of weakness, but it did not rest easy with me knowing that it may have given approval for the perpetrator's continued mistreatment towards other dark skin employees. This led me to contemplate whether other reasons could exist to explain the misconduct of others and could only find a couple.

Jealousy

The attempts by one employee to undermine another employee's work or achievements may be rooted in jealousy. Whilst working in an interim role, my manager would continuously refuse to help whenever I queried a process or sought general guidance to familiarise myself with the organisation's outdated systems. *'You should know'* or *'Get on with it, you're paid enough'* were the staple remarks which certainly did not encourage team building, but it took the display of competence in a challenging situation for the line manager to change their opinion of me. They apologised and admitted to being jealous of my skills which they perceived themself to lack. Yet a temporary transfer to other departments to gain the skill or a training course would have remedied their confidence problem.

In another example, it took for a senior manager to inform me of the extent of another manager's jealousy. *'Everyone knows that it is you and not them who manages the office'*. The thought had never crossed my mind at the time which may reflect an ignorance, but my priorities had been focused elsewhere. On reflection of the statement, it suddenly became apparent why my unique problem-solving ideas that I had discussed with the manager as a sounding board, would find themselves slipping out of mouths of one of my peers from a different location during workgroup sessions. Once is a coincidence but frequently? It also explained why team building days had ceased. A colleague informed me that the events had not stopped but were quietly organised to coincide with my planned absence from the office. It provided the manager with the opportunity to demean and use me as the butt of their jokes at the events. It also explained why

153

the finance manager was so dismissive whenever I expressed concerns about the sudden inability to balance my meticulous finance records.

Personality

There are times when you just simply do not like a person, no matter how hard you try. I have collaborated with many great people, and unfortunately with some real nasty personalities. These characters typically abuse their position for their own benefit and are malicious towards their colleagues. These toxic characters need psychological help to deal with their insecurities and should be referred to Occupational Health for an assessment of fitness to work in an office or any other work environment. Seriously! In these situations, I was considered a threat for whatever warped reason. Maybe they feared my becoming their replacement in the job, or I had exposed their incompetence in certain work activities, which cannot be helped if you are to do a job properly.

I wish I had discovered the song *'Everyday'* by Dawin Hobbs featuring Michael McDonald sooner, as such inspirational words serves as mental preparation for dealing with these individuals. Whatever the reason for their behaviours, it cannot be ignored that such conduct, especially where it

154

becomes persistent and malicious, crosses the line of the workplace playground stupidity into one of racial discrimination. Far too many dark skin employees or contractors walk away from the bad conduct of other employees instead of challenging the problem because of the hurdles that must be overcome to achieve a fair outcome, as seen in earlier chapters. To effect workplace changes and the removal of this inequality, such conduct cannot be ignored and need to be brought to the attention of the organisation. Following the organisation's grievance procedure and if required, pursuing the matter to employment tribunal resolution is the right of all employees who receive less favourable treatment in the workplace.

There can be no doubt that the mistreatment of employees would have been a contributory factor in the current workplace exodus occurring in the UK. With modern technology creating easier opportunities for self- employment, there is no longer a need for people to be shackled to one organisation or career path.

'Work harder' were the precious words spoken by my parents as a form of encouragement for me to achieve a life better than their own. It was and continues to be a generational voice of encouragement filled with love and hope. These words are more of a blessing if not recognised previously, because all

the effort feeding and growing one's talent can find a new purpose online if rejected in the corporate world that we know. The additional advantage of this new way of achieving a decent income, is that there is no requirement to disclose personal information such as skin colour, or ethnicity, or age, or disability, or sexuality, or religion.

So, emancipate yourself from the mental slavery and the rituals that binds you from being yourself! Then go down on bended knee and express your gratitude to the Divine and let all those who came before you know that you will achieve, because you are possible and unique in your own way. Do as I do and blast your music system with the song *'You Know My Name'* by Tasha Cobbs Leonard featuring Jimmy Cravity or by any other artist for inspiration and importantly, know that you are not alone in your fight for equal treatment.

> *'No fire can burn me,*
> *No battle can turn me,*
> *No mountain can stop me,*
> *No giant can defeat me…….'*

Do you get it? Never stop being your authentic self. The harmful actions and behaviours by another towards you, is evidence that it is them and not you, who has a problem.

156

CHAPTER 13

Case Studies of Racism in the Workplace

This chapter contains my personal experiences of race discrimination in the workplace and provides general guidance on the associated laws. The aim of disclosing this information serves two objectives. The first is to provide insight of the workplace events that result in the complaints raised by dark skin employees. The context surrounding the behaviours resulting in the allegations, the management of the allegations and areas of the law in relation to the allegations, are presented. It is hoped that by shining a light on the 'mismanagement' of these incidents, organisations will ensure the appropriate measures are embedded so that no employees experience discrimination in the workplace.

The other objective of sharing these experiences is to provide employees who encounter similar problems with the know how to manage the process and the resources available to them. Providing guidance to both parties in the employment relationship will hopefully remove the barriers restricting

157

procedural fairness where appropriate so that just resolutions may be achieved. In turn, the parties will avoid the additional financial and reputational risk of an employment tribunal or any other law court action where matters remain unresolved. Hence the guidance provided at the beginning of this book, *'If you can't hear, you must feel'*.

The cases cover a variety of situations where I have used the most recent legislation, namely the Equality Act 2010, to interpret these experiences of less favourable treatment. Although I must advise that I am no employment lawyer and views on my interpretation of the law may or may not differ. However, I have made a slight change with the hope that a greater understanding of the victim's experiences is gained. The facts of the incidents remain true with the exception that all victims now have a white skin colour, and the dominant group are all dark skinned. This change serves one purpose only, and that is for you to get it.

Darks skin employees for example, will no doubt have experienced less favourable treatment in the workplace but may not know how best to approach the situation or indeed, may question the validity a problem. Conversely, white skin employees may view a problem as trivial especially where acts of gross misconduct may be hidden from view. The guidance provided with these cases alongside the less favourable treatment discussed in earlier chapters, will hopefully provide a better understanding of racism in the workplace, so that you all get it and eliminate discrimination once and for all.

There are no names attached to any individuals or organisations as to assign names may result in a possible disconnect from the victim's experiences, which defeats the objective of the disclosure. The nameless are intentional, not out of fear of any repercussion or retribution but because they are undeserving and shall remain in the cesspool where they belong.

On completion of walking in the victim's shoes, reflect upon how you can influence a change where the voices of all employees are heard? Influencing change in one person is better than none. Influencing a change within a workforce is a significant achievement, but influencing a change for all stakeholders, well that is just priceless. Be the person, the organisation to start this positive chain reaction.

So, get comfortable, cuppa at the ready and begin to read. I have injected some humour so that the experience is more palatable, which I hope will leave you enlightened.

Enjoy!!

Case Studies

1 – Public Service Discrimination

You find that you are unable to secure any of the jobs that you interview for on a weekly basis. Even your contacts and former associates who reach out to discuss new contract opportunities, fail to follow through on the arrangements discussed that you begin to believe that you may have been blacklisted. Noting that your rainy-day savings are no more, you turn to family members for interim support whilst you sign up to a public service for financial and employment assistance.

You meet with a dark skin advisor with whom you discuss all the actions and challenges encountered to obtain employment. Details of a medical condition diagnosed a year earlier is also disclosed. Whilst the symptoms created new challenges daily, you felt they should not significantly impede your chances of securing employment. Taking these factors into account, you and the adviser make an agreement of the actions you will continue to pursue to find employment. They assign you to a nearby office to discuss your weekly activities which you are required to record in the newly established online journal account.

The first meeting with your assigned dark skin male adviser is productive, discussing your list of job searches, interviews, and suggested jobs fairs to attend. He praises your proactiveness and dedication trying to find employment which he says is far greater than the efforts made by other claimants and encourages you to continue with your efforts. You attend a couple of jobs fairs but find that the organisations in attendance are only targeting jobs or training events at young people. So, you provide feedback to your adviser with the recommendation of creating job fairs for mature and experienced job hunters.

The adviser continues to provide you with constructive supportive at your weekly meetings before change occurs and you are assigned a new adviser. In the first meeting with the new dark skin female adviser, she instructs you to contact a specific recruitment agency every day in your search for work. Thinking that she was probably related to the agency owner who was in desperate need of new victims, you express concern that such a request could be perceived as biased and anticompetitive. You explain that you liaised with a variety of recruitment organisations daily in your search for work, as your journal records reflected. The adviser is dismissive of your comments and tells you that you must do as you are told. The adviser then informs you of a new requirement for you to attend visits at their convenience and availability. Knowing these visits should occur every two weeks, you mention this to the adviser who repeats that they will occur whenever they had availability. You knew this would mean being available at their beck and call, and on leaving the appointment you knew this was just the beginning of a difficult relationship.

Within days you receive a text message to check your online journal for messages and see that the adviser has instructed you to update your curriculum vitae (cv) because in their view, it needed neatening up and shortening to two pages. The adviser instructs you contact a department who specialises in providing this type of service to jobhunters. Having updated your cv a few months previous which had been placed on your journal, you knew the document only superseded the standard by a couple of lines and was not the cause of the lack of job success. That said, you saw no harm in obtaining a different perspective on your cv but calls and emails to the contact details provided yielded no response from the local service. Instead, a specialist from the southern based office reaches out to provide you with guidance.

On time for your second appointment which takes place less than 14 days since your last visit, the advisor keeps you waiting. They have not been detained by another claimant because you see her at the desk chatting to colleagues and tinkering away at their keyboard. So, while you are kept waiting, you check your phone for feedback on the previous day's job interviews and see another interview request which makes you smile. When called to take a seat at the adviser's desk you hear them say on your approach, '*Oh gosh, you look as if you've gotten out of the wrong side of the bed this morning*'. The remark makes you stop in your tracks because you know that you were looking and feeling so damn fine. Politely, you respond by greeting the advisor with a '*Good Morning*' before letting them know that you had a great night's rest and had no difficulty getting out of your bed. Sitting in the chair, you wonder why they were deliberately being rude, but you were not going to allow them to dampen your good mood and wait for them to continue.

Not yet done with the '*bitchimgonnafrigupyourday*' attitude, the adviser tells you that the original commitment agreed with the service required updating. The new commitments needed your approval within 7 days, otherwise your claim would be cancelled. You knew this would mean that you would no longer be in receipt of the financial and healthcare support currently relied upon and so you ask the advisor why the need to revise the commitments. They tell you that advisors are expected to update the agreement at each visit, which was news to you and implied that your former adviser had failed to do their job properly.

To begin, the advisor asks whether you had a favourite recruitment agency that you contacted daily. A slightly different question to the one posed at your last visit, but still inferring a bias and so you reiterate your previous answer. The adviser again repeats their instructions for you to contact a favourite agency daily. Clearly unaware of how agencies function, you object to the unreasonable instruction but are told to do it anyway because '*you are not doing enough*'. Wow! You ask the adviser to explain their remark, but she ignores you.

Next, the adviser tells you that they have the right to book you onto any job fair event organised by the centre and that you must attend them otherwise your claim will be cancelled. Having already provided feedback on the centre's activities, you knew such a demand was unreasonable if events failed to cater to mature and experienced job hunters. Articulating your concerns

164

again served no purpose because you are again told '*You are not doing enough*'. Again, you ask the adviser to elaborate on their comments, but they surprise you by asking you in a loud voice not to shout. You respond that you were in no way shouting but asking a straightforward question to which you wanted a response, but again you are ignored.

Your commute time to a workplace is next on the agenda, with the adviser deciding that the existing agreed time limit required adjustment to the maximum. They explain that extending the commute time would provide ample scope for you to reach any workplace destination. The original commitment took account of your medical condition and the need for reasonable adjustments to protect your wellbeing. Yet once again, your objections to the changes which were negligible, is disregarded. The adviser comments that you will have plenty of time to get to the front door of a workplace, so you had no excuse. Wow!

Confirming that you had a degree to the next question posed, you knew the adviser was being obnoxious given their online instruction about updating your cv. Their next demand is that you sign up to an apprenticeship scheme offered by the Civil Service, the NHS, and the police services so that you can get trained into a job. The adviser tells you that as you were familiar with typing, any data entry or any clerical work would be an easy enough job for you. In disbelief, you ask whether they were joking, but they glare at you when responding that they were not. So, you sarcastically remark that you could always stack shelves at a famous grocery food store or even lecture, given that these were one off experience that you would never again entertain. The adviser jumps on your retort by asking if you had ever lectured before to which you confirm that you had done so, once as a student several years ago. They reply by saying that you could lecture and do an apprenticeship.

Exasperated with how events were unfolding, you begin to explain to the adviser in the hope they had an element of comprehension, that your challenges were not created by inactivity. The adviser is not interested and tells you that '*You've not been doing a good job of it then have you? Otherwise, you'd have a job by now*'. Amazed at your level of self-control you hear the adviser threaten to cancel your claim again if you refused to accept the new commitment which would be sent to your online account for approval. You ask the adviser to ensure that they also sent details of the appeal process against the

166

unilaterally imposed changes that were both unethical and biased, before departing from the centre.

Within days, you notice several emails from unfamiliar recruitment organisations about vacancies in sectors that you had not worked in since leaving school. You wondered why you were suddenly the recipient of these emails when you were registered with numerous jobsites specifically catering to your profession. When you hit the spam button to delete the emails from your inbox, you are prompted to remove them using the unsubscribe option. You follow the instruction without realising that you had not registered with these sites in the first instance.

Then you receive an email from the famous grocery store you had sarcastically referenced in the last meeting with the adviser and again you absentmindedly unsubscribe from their emails. Two days later, you receive another email from an unknown recruitment organisation on the coast, seeking a lecturer for a further educational establishment some 90 minutes away from your home. The penny finally drops, and all begins to make sense. The final cherry on top is the plethora of penis enlargement products and foreign brides for purchase emails which would not normally reach your email inbox unless you had ventured upon these types of sites online. You guessed the

167

adviser must have had difficulty deciding which way you swung and was being courteous in proving you with options.

Your attention is taken away from the adviser's antics due to family bereavements but when you finally get around to checking your journal messages, you find that your claim has been cancelled. The date of the cancellation occurred ten days after your last meeting with the adviser because you had refused to relinquish the control of your life into their incompetent hands by signing the new commitment. Yet you also notice an entry in the journal made by the adviser, five days after your initial meeting with her and one day after her instruction for you to update your cv. The entry showed that the adviser had cancelled your claim. This did not make any sense given that the cancellation occurred ten days after your last visit to the service which had taken place mid-month. Why then would the adviser cancel your claim on two separate occasions, one with notice and the other without notice, within days of your visits? Wow!

Continuing to scroll through journal messages noting the job events recorded by the centre, you see the entries posted by the adviser. The first entry was posted a day or two after your last visit, instructing you to contact them if you did not intend to attend your appointments, as it was the *'polite thing to do'*.

Given that the next appointment would have occurred two weeks from the last, this pre-emptive statement made you believe that the adviser was definitely an expert in their field. The job fair organised with the famous grocery store also grabs your attention. The entry was posted early in the morning by the adviser that requested interested parties to make contact '*to get that job!!*' By early evening of the same day, your claim had been cancelled. It was too coincidental that the common link connecting the sudden surge of the unsolicited job emails direct to your personal email account and the job fair event with the famous grocery store, was your adviser.

Accessing the public service's website in search for complaints forms, you find only a Reconsideration of Your Claim form. So, you make a call to the data protection body about the non-consensual disclosure of your personal data, and they provide guidance on the action to take. You then make a call to the equality regulatory body responsible for human rights and log your complaint in addition to utilising their template complaint letters to raise a complaint to the public service. On completing the reconsideration form and two letters of complaints, you hand deliver the letters to the public service's

169

local office and email the Data Protection controller at the government department accountable for the public service.

Whilst waiting for responses to your complaints, you contact the equality advisory service to ascertain the exact nature of the support they were willing to provide. Unfortunately, you find that no one person has been assigned to your query and your communications are passed from pillar to post. The standard response that you receive is to obtain legal advice from a lawyer as any referral to the main body can only be achieved if the complaint is relevant to their strategic aim. You ask for clarification of the strategic aim given that the organisation was established to remove inequality from society, but none is forthcoming. Your numerous attempts to acquire constructive support ends on the realisation that the once powerful kick ass organisation was no more. Conversely, the data service express concern and would act on your behalf, although they too had limitations due to current budget constraints.

Two months and still no acknowledgement or response to your complaints from the public service, you email the data protection controller seeking an update. You are informed that your complaint had been forwarded to the relevant person but no more. The adviser who answers your call to the public service, checks their record and informs you that your complaint letters and reconsideration form had been placed on the internal IT system upside down making it difficult for anyone to read. The advisor logs a priority request for action to the northern office and apologises to you for the delay.

Deciding enough was enough, you contact your locally elected member of parliament and provide details about your complaint. You do the same with the law service who are only able to support in some areas of your complaint due to resource limitations. You are happy to relinquish control of this situation as the rules governing public protection was no more and had been replaced by devilish control games.

Four months after the claim was cancelled, you receive notification from the local member of parliament that your case had been dealt with and that you should receive a response from the public service. When you eventually receive notification to check your journal, you find a letter from an unnamed Office Manager confirming that your claim should not have been closed on the date following your first meeting with the adviser and would be reinstated. No explanation is provided on why your claim had been closed twice. You find yourself having to chase for the full payments owed to you and for the responses to your complaints.

Six months after handing the service your complaint letters, you finally receive another response. The letter is not from the Data Protection Controller responsible for investigating the organisation's data breaches, nor from a senior postholder addressing the discrimination issues raised. The letter is from the adviser's Team Leader, who having spoken to the adviser and carried out an investigation, was unable to explain the reason for the unwanted emails you had received. They claim that none of the websites could be accessed from the organisation's system. They also inform you that the adviser had failed to advise you of your right to seek a second opinion when they '*explored*' the changes to your commitment agreement. Explored? You see that a due process had not been conducted with any impartial investigation into the suspected abuse of your personal data. The no access explanation made no sense given that the local office arranged regular job and training events with local partners to which the adviser had access. Their responsibilities also required a compliance with the legal duties of discrimination law, which was not evident by the adviser's attitude towards you.

When the spam emails began to occur, you had conducted a historical search of your inbox and outbox to establish whether you had made any former contact with the organisations who had sent the unsolicited emails. You knew that your cv did not reference any experience of lecturing, night care work, shelf stacking, data entry, mail order bride or any other jobs that the adviser deemed you suitable to secure. Your search confirmed what you already knew that you had only signed up to a selection of job sites that catered to your niche. It was difficult to ignore that the timing of all the newly unsolicited emails for these new job types were exactly the same as those which the adviser had ordered you to apply for at your second meeting.

However, it was the email from another unknown organisation that left you astounded. The email confirmed that your personal details had been removed from the company's website, *'as you had requested'*. Someone was clearly attempting to cover their tracks and to destroy any evidence of their wrongdoing. Through email or telephone communication, you contact the organisations seeking to learn how they had acquired your personal data. All replies from six of the organisations contacted stated that the information had been obtained from your cv posted on a specific job site. There was

173

no variation in the websites they had all allegedly accessed, which was most unusual.

Your direct emails to the sender of the lecturing roles go unanswered initially that you resort to connecting with them through another means. You finally receive a response, and they too confirm the same job site as those other organisations. They also block all further communications with you. Intriguingly, when contacting the famous grocery store, you are passed around by recruiters before the data controller provides you with secure access to a porthole to read their response to your complaint. On access, you find no response waiting and all future attempts to communicate with the organisation also goes unanswered.

You decide to take time out to contemplate your next course of action, which is likely to be another referral to the office governing data protection given your collated evidence. The discriminatory conduct remains outstanding and given the dismissive approach taken with your complaint, legal action is the only recourse available to you.

The Law

The European Convention for the Protection of Human Rights and Fundamental Freedom (EHRC), advocates that all people have rights to life, appropriate treatment, and protection in living life. The UK Human Rights Act 1998 came into effect in 2000 which embeds the Convention Rights and provides an easier means for challenges of Human Rights issues to be dealt with in UK.

Human Rights is embedded into all UK laws that governs our everyday life as seen with the discrimination legislation. Part One of the Equality Act 2010 pertains to the socio-economic inequalities which places a duty on public authorities to have a due regard to the EHRC when exercising its function. Authorities must do this in such a way that reduces inequalities of outcome to those already disadvantaged socially and economically.

Part Two of the Equality Act relates to the prohibited conduct and the protected characteristics definitions. Direct discrimination is defined as where one person treats another person less favourably or would treat them less favourably, because of a protected characteristic. The less favourable treatment also includes segregating a person from others.

175

Indirect discrimination is defined as the provision, criteria or practice that is equally applied to all people but causes disadvantages to a person or group who has a protected characteristic when compared to others. Where the provision, criteria or practice cannot be shown to be a proportionate means of achieving a legitimate aim, then it is deemed to be unlawful.

Harassment is defined as the unwanted conduct which has the purpose of violating a person's dignity or creating an intimidating, hostile, degrading, humiliating or offensive environment. Victimisation is also contained in the Act and relates to a person who is caused a detriment because they have or are believed to have initiated or participated in the formal processes in good faith.

The Prohibition of Slavery and Forced Labour is contained within Article 4 of ECHR which is embedded within the UK's, the Modern-Day Slavery Act 2015. The Equality and Human Rights Commission define modern day slavery as an individual being forced to do work that they have not agreed to and is threatened with punishment on refusal.

Article 8 of the EHRC relates to the Right to Respect for Private and Family Life. Given the explosion of digital platforms, the UK's legislation has been extended to include the

176

respect for private correspondence including emails. This increasing challenge is policed by the UK's Information Commissioners Office who oversees the current General Data Protection Regulations (GDPR) 2018 which replaced the former Data Protection Act 1998.

The above section briefly sets out how European and UK laws are entwined covering all aspects of valuing and protecting human life. Reference to the individual laws and regulations will now be contrasted with your experience at the public service organisation.

Forced Labour

The conduct of the adviser ordering you to apply for jobs and apprenticeships, even attending job fare events targeted at young people, may not appear unreasonable. Their objective may have been to take all necessary steps to return you to the working world so that you were no longer reliant upon the public support service, a service that your tax contributions had aided for a few decades. It is possible they felt that as a generation X member, their duty was to determine your career path and mitigate the mass workplace exodus taking place. Apprenticeships were, after all, the new venture for mature people seeking to fulfil their personal ambitions. Had a choice option been presented to you, then architecture, master joinery or contortionism would have been the desired apprenticeship options pursued.

Failing to discuss your aspirations and insisting instead to control your next employment opportunity, their actions, whether knowingly or otherwise, could be viewed as labour being forced upon you. The threat to cancel your claim if non-compliant, supports the definition of the modern slavery where you are being required to perform a job that is forced upon you without any regard to your skills or wellbeing. This Hobson's Choice situation shows an intent to humble you, for some unknown reason. Their intention to control your prospects are further reflected by their actions pertaining to your personal data.

Personal Data Protection

Any personal data obtained by the public service must have a specified and lawful purpose and used with the consent of the person to whom the data relates. More specifically, personal data must be kept secure so that it is protected against unlawful or unauthorised processing, access, loss, destruction, or damage. When a person objects to how their data is being processed, the requirement on public organisations is for the appointed Data

Controller of the organisation to respond within 20 working days to the complaint, enabling sufficient time for appropriate investigations to be conducted.

At no time during your connection with the public service was you informed that your personal data would be disclosed to third party organisations without your explicit permission. Advisers tended to recommend rather than act on a service user's behalf, as reflected with the cv update 'request'. However, your own investigation strongly indicated that your personal information had been disclosed without your consent. The evidence of having no prior connection with the organisations and the dates of their unsolicited communications points towards unlawful conduct being at play.

Questioning the organisations about the acquisition of your personal data yielded equivocal or evasive responses. Furthermore, the sectors and nature of work to which their emails related, were not comparable to your specialism and therefore your cv would not have appeared in their online searches. The email to you from an unknown organisation confirming the deletion of your data that you personally had not requested, further confirms your suspicions. The public service's letter written by a Team Leader and not a designated Data

179

Controller specialist, fails to demonstrate impartiality and a robust exploration of the data breaches, which makes for an extremely serious operational concern.

The Adviser's Behaviour

It is not unreasonable to expect a civil and reasonable level of service from a public service when seeking their assistance. Especially as most of these services have additional responsibilities pertaining to prohibited conduct when providing a service to the public. You are aware that had an employee displayed discriminatory behaviours in any other workplace, then they would have been subjected to formal action and possibly dismissal.

Instead of offering quality advice, the inflexible conduct of the adviser encompasses the definitions of discrimination with acts of rudeness, demeaning and derogatory remarks. Your character was judged not by your efforts seeking employment but on the opinion of the adviser. This resulted in targeted actions with your claim being closed twice within days of both your meetings with them. Their remarks of you not doing enough to find employment when the contrary was clearly evidenced, highlighted their bias. A stereotypical view of laziness and you sponging off the government for an income, was being

180

conveyed. This would explain why your challenge to the adviser's *'not doing enough'* remarks were met with silence in all instances, which inferred discrimination. To further accuse you of shouting implies that you were being aggressive thereby meeting their biased opinion of you having an aggressive trait which necessitated their need to control and retain a perceived superiority over you.

Discrimination

It is noted that anything done by the perpetrator of the unfair act in the course of their employment towards a service user, is treated as also being done by the organisation. As such the organisation will be held liable for the adviser's actions. Claims of ignorance or lack of understanding of the organisation's responsibilities when dealing with a service user who has a protected characteristic when compared to another who does not, will be no excuse or absolve the public organisation of its legal duties.

It may be argued that the treatment that you experienced by the adviser is one that is consistently and universally adopted by all advisers employed to provide this type of employment service throughout the UK. This would mean that the government and those leaders presiding over the public service approve of such conduct by their workforce, especially if it forms part of a strategy to get the unemployed back into work.

Disability

A person who has a mental or physical impairment that has a substantial and long-term adverse effect on them to carry out normal day to day activities is considered to have a disability. An impairment is usually one that lasts for a period of more than twelve months and so there is an expectation to make reasonable adjustments to support a person with a disability, where possible.

Public services are obliged to protect service users from being caused any detriment when providing a service. By imposing the standard rule applied to all general service users and disregarding a person's disability when making decisions will be viewed as less favourable treatment. Within a legal setting, details of your disability would need to be disclosed so that a due process on the extent of the inhibiting factors can be considered for the assessment of the award.

It is possible that the public service's objective was to secure you employment which fulfilled their 'by any means necessary' strategy. This may be viewed as indirectly discriminatory towards disabled service users given that it fails to take account of individual disabilities. The public service would need to evidence that the disadvantage would impact only a small proportion of people with a particular disability when compared to other disabled individuals.

Age

The less favourable treatment in the type of work that you were ordered to secure reflected the old stereotype of being aged and ~~incontinent~~ incompetent. A referral to a service that provided job support to experienced and mature adults returning to the workplace would have been a reasonable option rather than to assume that you no longer had neither the capacity or capability to think or to function as a human being.

It is possible that the public service believed there was a genuine occupational requirement for people over a certain age to stack shelves in food stores. They may have viewed the mature unemployed as best suited for such work which fulfilled a strategic aim of no other age group wanting the frigging jobs. However, the public service would need to be mindful of forcing mature people into such jobs as it may lead to significant complaints from the famous grocery food store. Staff turnover will be high due to absences caused by health conditions of rheumatoid arthritis, hip replacement surgery or the constant loss of hearing aids in the middle isles. Customer complaints may

183

also increase because of the menopausal employee who inadvertently cooks the food in the chiller cabinets whenever she walks by, or the fresh fruit and vegetable left sautéed when restocked.

Race

The difference in treatment because of a person's skin colour, nationality, ethnic or national origin is not easily evidenced until one considers the conduct of the adviser. The repeated statements of *'you are not doing enough'* without explanation was not the constructive support the service is required to provide, neither is imposing a control mechanism that denied you free will and punished with hardship if you refused. You were expected to be compliant to the new arrangement and be without a voice as your needs or concerns did not matter.

The extent of the abuse included cancelling your claim twice which extended to the disclosure of your personal data to third party organisations. The public service confirmed in two separate correspondences that the adviser had been wrong to take specific actions with your claim. Given the lack of an impartial response to your data breach concerns and the absence of a response regarding the adviser's discriminatory behaviour, these facts indicates that on a balance of probability, that you were a victim of discrimination by the public service because of your skin colour.

Practical Advice

Where service users find their assigned adviser behaves in a similar manner as that outlined above, whether rude, threatening or attempts to control your employment opportunities instead of providing you with constructive support, then immediately insist upon speaking to a manager. In taking this stance immediately, you are unlikely to endure any further challenges as the manager is obliged to resolve matters promptly. You also have the right to demand being assigned to a different adviser if the one allocated to you is ineffective.

Respectful consideration for your personal circumstances and timely complaint resolution standards does not currently exist within this public service. Circumventing their own rules means that complaints go unactioned for months or even years which is both unethical and unprofessional. The traditional investigatory standards of acknowledging complaints within two working day and receiving a full response to your complaint or a holding letter within ten working days of receipt, is no more. Therefore, should you discover that your claim has been cancelled then you should reapply for a new claim in addition to completing a Reconsideration of My Claim form. Completing a new claim will ensure that you are not left without financial support for too long whereas waiting on the outcome of a reconsideration will take months beyond their stipulated timeframe of three months.

Finally, seek legal advice. Free advice can be obtained from law centres around the UK regions or from local citizens advice bureaux. The legal and benefits specialist may act on your behalf to resolve a problem with your claim, or any sanctions imposed by the public service, promptly. Contacting your local member of parliament will also be more effective than contacting certain regulatory organisations whose strategic purpose of playing with an abacus has superseded its established legal duties. Let us all hope that any governments change will restore the professional standards within this and other public services to their former glory and purpose.

As for this public service, there is most definitely a need for transformation. Those identified power mad occupants in roles pretending to be employment specialists and who have yet to be dismissed, must be redeployed into new positions. The partnership with the famous grocery food store makes this an

186

ideal contender for the redeployed, so that all the customer facing and shelf stacking vacancies around the country are no more. This recommendation is well intended as it will enable this selection of employees who have damaged the reputation of the public organisation, to learn the most fundamental skills of customer service and catering to the needs of the public with courtesy and respect. Vacancies arising from this cleansing exercise may be backfilled by the job hunters ready to return to employment following their earlier exodus, or by those recruitment agency consultants who are more apt at coordinating appropriate employment opportunities for job hunters. Seriously, transform this service!

2 – The Interview

Invited to an interview for a junior management position where you are required to do a 10-minute presentation, you spend many hours researching the employing organisation and preparing for the interview. Dressed professionally, you arrive 10 minutes early for the interview and so you engage in a polite conversation with the dark-skinned receptionist about a television programme that you both had watched the night before.

Called into a meeting room to begin the interview, the two dark skin panel members rise from their chairs to greet you. Reaching out your arm, you shake the hand of the male panel member who warmly welcomes you to the interview. He introduces himself before turning to introduce his female colleague whom you turn towards offering your hand and hearing yourself say '*I'm pleased to meet you*', only to find your hand floating in cold air with icicles beginning to form at your fingertips. You catch the female screwing up her face as if she could smell excrement on you, but you knew that was impossible because you had emptied your favourite perfume all over that morning. An indecipherable mumble is released from the panel member's lips and after an uncomfortable minute, you return the

188

now frozen hand to the side of your body. Sitting down in the waiting chair to begin the interview, you hope and pray that your hand does not hit the chair and smash to pieces.

The male interviewer begins to ask you questions which you answer comfortably although you notice that his colleague is not making any eye contact with you or taking any notes but is sat in her chair facing the side profile of her colleague. When it is the female's turn to ask questions, they do so by directing all their questions towards the side profile of her colleague, who is busy writing. Clearly there was something that had her transfixed and so you conclude that he probably had a wax build up in his ear. Throughout your presentation, the female continues to ignore you and busy herself twirling in her chair like a toddler who has just discovered the wonders of a merry go round that you expect to hear a '*weeeeeee*' at any minute.

Then you hear the female tutting, huffing, and puffing, waiting for the presentation to end so that she could no doubt grab herself something to suck on. Kids!! You bring your presentation to an end quickly and as no final questions are asked, you politely say your goodbyes, without shaking any hands and depart never wishing to entertain that organisation again. As expected, you receive a brief communication that

189

confirms that you were unsuccessful on this occasion, as if you would give them another opportunity.

Interview

The interview panel members are employees who represent the organisation and provide the opportunity to make a first impression on candidates who wish to enter their employ. Panel members not only provide the doorway into the organisation, but they are also a reflection of the culture and personalities contained within. First impressions work both ways in this ritual of suitability and will leave a lasting effect on candidates which is why up to date interview skills and equality training is essential for panel members.

Behaviour

Had the female panel member behaved in an ethical manner and remained cordial throughout the interview ritual, you would have been none the wiser about their personal view of you. Their behaviour of displaying their disgust towards you, refusing to shake your hand, and ignoring you throughout the duration of the interview displayed a hostility towards you that can only be interpreted as '*I don't care what you have, I don't want it*'. Requesting a copy of the interview score sheet to see how your performance and ethnicity compared to other candidates may have highlighted this bias and explained this unfair treatment.

Speculating on the female interviewer's conduct, this could possibly be explained by some form of medication that had taken effect and suddenly transformed their wonderful personality. Or it is possible that it was they and not you, who had the excrement on their persons. Either way, it fails to provide a reasonable explanation for the unexpected and unprofessional treatment that you received. The only question to ask in such situations is whether you would have been treated differently by the female panel member if you had shared the same skin colour? Unless they were also obnoxious to other interviewees, then the reason for the behaviour is because of your skin colour.

It is always worth remembering in these situations that any rejection is for your protection and better opportunities will always come your way.

191

3 – Mismanaged Recruitment

Contracting through a recruitment agency for several months, you finally begin to see the progress of your hard work within a client organisation. Operating in a department that outsources its services, you are the only white skin person operating in a managerial role. The good working relationships established with co-workers has helped you to resolve many employee issues which had led you to create an improvement strategy for the designated business.

With yet another contract extension you are asked to support a further two businesses where travel expenses would be met, and so you agree and reorganise your time to deliver the support. You discover shortly afterwards that your line manager who had recruited you into the role, would soon be departing the organisation due to a restructure programme. Rumours abound that your line manager had applied for the senior role heading the department but had lost out to the current head of the department who allegedly wrote the job description for the new position.

You were aware of such unethical practices within this sector and knew of a similar event occurring a few years earlier in another similar contract. The preferred candidate for a

192

leadership position in that instance had also been ousted from the role by an inexperienced competitor. You preferred not to engage in any office politics being an interim worker and avoided judging situations, even though on this occasion, the successful candidate and your new line manager is the only senior manager in the team that you had yet to meet. The negative opinion from your colleagues makes you believe that it would be best to never meet them.

Supporting the other businesses proves challenging, especially when the assigned assistants are removed to resolve the problems in the hub arising from a badly managed restructure programme. Your travel expenses begin to build up and so you enquire about making expenses claims. This matter is eventually resolved with you providing details to your agency who in turn would obtain authorisation from your line manager prior to making a payment. However, your line manager is about to step out the door and their departing comments to you is to *'watch your back'*, explaining that the new line manager took exception to anyone who outshined them and that you were next in line on their attack list. You then learn that the line manager leaves with a 'redundancy package' even though they had less than two years of service with the organisation.

Your new line manager is also dark skin, but you have very little interaction with them and continue to work with your assigned business areas. One of which is having difficulty with a white skin contractor expressing inappropriate views resulting in fellow white skin employees complaining to their line manager. You provide instructions for the prompt removal of the contractor with an explanation of the behavioural problems to their recruitment organisation.

You finally meet the new line manager in a team meeting, but no discussion takes place to review your work or any challenges. A few weeks later, it is announced that the temporary role that you occupy is to be advertised in the search for a permanent placement. You encourage the dark skin assistants working alongside you to apply for the role. You also learn that your dark skin colleague supporting another business area on a contract, would also be throwing their hat into the ring. Knowing that your colleague had a wealth of experience working in various business sectors, you felt that the recruitment drive would be good practice for the assistants whom you felt were competent enough to do the job justice.

Your new line manager, who is the recruiting manager, decides to conduct a three-stage recruitment process starting with an online assessment a week before holding an assessment day which would finish with job interviews. Your colleague, however, mentions having difficulty completing the online assessment due to what they viewed to be an outdated test format.

On the day of the assessment and interview, you receive an angry call again from your colleague, this time to say they had not reached the interview stage. Following the assessment activity, the recruiting manager had informed your colleague that they had failed to demonstrate any competencies for the role and had failed in the online assessment. Given that your colleague was in the same role as you but within a different business area, the remark was considered deeply offensive. Your colleague also disclosed that two of the assessment moderators were senior managers who had recently been subjects of formal action where your colleague had presided over the cases. Doubting that they had received appropriate training for the event, your colleague suspected that the moderators' participation in the assessment was an opportunity to seek their revenge by assigning low scores to deny them the employment opportunity. Your colleague ends the conversation by telling you that they had no intention of returning to the workplace.

195

Concerned by these events, you email your line manager requesting an opportunity to discuss your now former colleague's comments. Arrangements are made to discuss them at a team project meeting being held the following day. In the project meeting whilst all attendees are present, your line manager announces the name of the selected candidate who had been made a provisional job offer and whom the line manager knew well having previously worked with them in another organisation. The manager then proudly announces to the assistant who was one of the candidates in the recruitment event, that they had not secured the role but had performed well throughout the event. Oblivious to the shocked expressions around the room, the manager continues to sing their own praises of conducting the candidate shifting and selection for interview alone and were pleased to have managed the task over two evenings.

Once the meeting room is cleared, with only the recruitment manager responsible for administering the recruitment process present, you raise your concerns to the manager about the earlier disclosure and the perceived bias raised by the former colleague, which all had countered best practices. You suggest the rerunning of the process given these concerns to which the manager says that they would consider your suggestion.

A few days later whilst in a senior leadership meeting to present data on your business area activities, a senior manager asks why a high percentage of the organisation's discriminations claims have occurred in one of your business areas. Unprepared for the question, you confirm being unaware of such problems, as only one case which had been discussed, existed in your areas. You offer to investigate and provide feedback for the next meeting but questioned how they had formed such an opinion. The senior manager tells you that your line manager had drawn the problem to their attention. The research into the discrimination claim supports your statement to the senior manager and when despatching a response by email, you draw their attention to the offending business areas responsible for the high case levels and offer some practical guidance on addressing the issues.

On learning of your line manager's intention to continue the recruitment process on your day off work, you despatch an email suggesting that they conducted an impact assessment to ensure that no unfair acts had occurred in the process before the activity was resumed. Your manager agrees to this suggestion in

197

their response. However, on your return to the office, you learn from an assistant that the manager had 'a tantrum' in front of all your colleagues on receipt of your email. The assistant had been disgusted by the unprofessional conduct that included screaming disparaging comments that they felt you should be informed.

At the next full team meeting the person conducting the impact assessment reports that whilst some issues of bias had occurred in the recruitment process, they felt that no racial discrimination had taken place. They had reached this conclusion because there was no guidance on the regulatory bodies' website to show that the manager shifting applications alone was unfair. In disbelief, you begin to inform the reporter that their findings were incorrect, but the manager interrupts you with their question to learn the reason for your interest in the recruitment exercise. As you begin to explain, you hear a colleague who had previously been friendly, make a sarcastic remark and so you say nothing further on the matter. In fact, no other team member openly expresses a view about the recruitment process, which convinces you that you had entered the twilight zone.

You take a couple of days off work and make your weekly contact to the recruitment consultant who had placed you in the

~~lion's den~~ contract and provide the latest update on your eagerness to leave. You also remind them that the manager has continually failed to approve your weekly time sheets meaning you had not been paid for more than a month. The consultant promises to pursue this, and your expenses claims with the line manager and copies the sent emails to you. You note however that the contracted travel expenses incurred is not mentioned in the communication but hope that they too will be approved.

Visiting the office of one of the businesses, you greet two colleagues who had attended the team meeting the previous week. Whilst you had previously enjoyed friendly conversations with them, your greeting goes unanswered. Repeating the greeting, you hear them reluctantly mumble in response. You learn from one of the business managers that your colleagues were on site to deliver an event which derived from the strategy and action plan you had produced to improve service standards in the business area. Realising this was not a one-off situation and other events had occurred without your knowledge, you finally grasp the true meaning of 'teamwork'.

You mention the behaviour of your colleagues to the report writer and question the reason for the change in attitude towards you. The report writer responds that the line manager had

199

informed your colleagues that you had made derogatory comments about their abilities to do their jobs. You stress having done nothing of the sorts and would speak with them on your next visit to the hub, but the report writer offers to do the honours on your behalf when they returned to the hub later in the day.

You return to your desk to find that you are copied into an email from your manager to the senior management team. It relays a solicitor's views about a weak employment tribunal claim in your business area but expressed concerns about a possible inference of discrimination by business managers. The email also referenced the manager's intention to complete the recruitment activity having found no race discrimination in the process.

Responding to the email, you clarify that the solicitor's concern about inference was in fact related to the activities of the recruitment organisation and not those of the business managers. You also provide clarification on the good practice methods in recruitment and how the informal activities adopted would have an impact on candidates with a protected characteristic which countered the organisation's equality duty.

The senior manager responds asking that your manager resolves the issue directly with you. In a telephone call your line manager accuses you of being responsible for segregation. Shocked by their comment, you ask them to clarify the remark as they possibly intended to say segmentation, as your strategy had highlighted this as a potential problem in one of the businesses. However, your manager insists that they meant exactly what they said, segregation. You hear them say that your suggestion some months previously of promoting the advisers temporarily until your replacement was in post had been a good idea that they now intended to follow through on it. Therefore, your services were no longer be required and your departure would be expected in a week.

Even after leaving the client organisation, your time sheets still take a long time to be approved by the manager. Your travel expenses, which only covered car parking costs and not mileage, are not approved, even though your renewed contracts expressed they would be payable. Your complaints to the recruitment agency, whilst sympathetic to your plight, yields no outcome after months of chasing.

Several months later, you receive a call from a recruitment consultant asking you to apply for an interim role believing your skills were a perfect match for the post. The recruiting manager heading a newly restructured service, was experiencing difficulties finding the right candidate for the role and had spent several months in their search. During the conversation you learn the name of the recruiting manager and politely make your excuses to quickly bring the conversation to an end. You wondered for a minute whether the recruitment consultant would let your former line manager know that they had reached out to you about the vacancy.

Agency Worker Regulations (2010)

An agency worker who secures temporary employment at an organisation through a recruitment agency, is deemed to be an employee of the recruitment agency. The arrangement means working under the temporary supervision and direction of the hiring organisation.

The Agency Worker Regulations 2010 protects agency workers from being treated less favourably when compared to permanent employees in the hiring organisation. From the start of the temporary employment, agency workers have rights to apply for any permanent vacancies and have access to any basic benefit provided to employees through collective agreement such as canteen and bathroom facilities. After a qualifying period of 12 weeks, agency workers are entitled to equal treatment to some of the same basic working conditions of employment as an employee. These are the basic collective agreements incorporated into the contracts of employees such as pay, working time, annual leave, and rest breaks.

Where an agency worker suspects a breach to their contract has occurred, they may seek an explanation from the agency who is obliged to provide a response within 28 days. This may entail the agency contacting the hiring organisation for information. Where no response is forthcoming, the agency worker may redirect their request to the hiring organisation who also has 28 days to respond. Where matter remain unresolved, the agency worker may make a claim to an employment tribunal within 3 months from when the breach occurred. The recruitment agency and or the hiring organisation will be held liable for breaching the agency worker's contract.

Whilst you had recourse to make a claim to the employment tribunal due to the non-payment of your travel expenses, which was a written term of your renewed contract, and the conduct of staff members at the hiring organisation, you chose to take no action. Likewise, it is noted that the recruitment agency failed to provide you with an explanation for the mistreatment that you

203

received from the hiring organisation. Only an employment tribunal could determine whether the less favourable treatment that you received from both the recruiting and hiring organisations were because of your skin colour and which of the two to hold accountable for the discrimination. That said, one can presume that if the recruitment agency had followed the due process and requested but received no response from the hiring organisation to your complaints, then the absence of a response infers discrimination by the hiring organisation.

Equality Duty

The Equality Act 2010 places a responsibility on public sector organisations to have due regard when carrying out its functions with the purpose of: eliminating discrimination, harassment, victimisation, and any other prohibited conduct. Notably, they must advance equality of opportunity between people who do not share the same protected characteristics and foster good relations between them. Tackling prejudices and promoting understanding between those different groups who have and do not have a protected characteristic is an essential requirement.

The accountability of ensuring the equality duty is adhered within organisations rests with the senior executive and managers of the organisation. They are required to monitor and improve upon processes, systems, and practices within the organisation to remove any identifiable barriers of inequality. In this instance, the identified inequality brought to the attention of the senior manager was the recruitment process and the high levels of discrimination complaints. Had the senior manager understood their responsibility to the Equality Duty, the line manager as the head of the department would have been required to explain the organisation's failure to meet the legal duty and the constructive measures planned to resolve and prevent any future problems. Instead, the senior manager saw two managers squabbling rather than the serious nature of the issue in debate and so delegated their responsibility to the perpetrator and enabler of the unjust acts.

Recruitment

The organisation's recruitment practices appeared not to have met best practices given the concerns expressed by your colleague about the time restrictions imposed on the online assessment and the moderators involved in the day assessment. The additional issues of the candidate selection methods, the appointment of the preferred candidate and the lack of respect shown to the assistant as a candidate of the process, tended to support the concerns raised.

The online assessment tool utilised by the organisation was considered outdated by your colleague. Whether this was because of the assessment form content or format, or in the way it was administered e.g., time restrictions, it was perceived to have restricted candidates with a neurological disability.

The use of suspected untrained moderators in a recruitment assessment may be viewed as biased, where the scoring of the assessment criteria is unfairly judged. Given the accessible resources available to the organisation, the failure of the recruiting manager to utilise the interview panel members or the HR team in the candidate sifting and selection process may also be viewed as biased. The non-disclosure of the manager's former association with the preferred candidate is a conflict-of-interest concern, and the public disclosure of the assistant's interview outcome are all evidence of an ill managed recruitment drive.

The impact assessment report confirmed 'accepted' biases in the recruitment process. It also concluded that no racial discrimination had occurred but made no reference to the other protected characteristics defined by the Equality Act.

Line Manager & Colleagues' Behaviours

Irrespective of the seniority of the position held, all managers are employees of the organisation and their actions when carrying out their duties, are deemed to be those of the organisation. As a result of you expressing concerns about the recruitment process adopted by the recruiting manager, they in turn quickly destroyed any established credibility that you had achieved within the team.

The first act was the blind-siding remarks from the senior manager, followed by continual misinformation of discrimination in your business areas which you were having to constantly correct and defend. This can be viewed as a deliberate attempt to undermine your abilities in front of senior personnel. The reported outburst and character assassination to fellow colleagues followed by the untruths spoken about your colleagues' capabilities, enabled the destruction of any established trust and cordial cooperation resulting in your exclusion from key events occurring in your business areas and the isolation from your colleagues. This is finally topped with the accusation of segregation being levied against you and following your departure from the organisation, the delayed authorisation of timesheets and the non-authorisation of your travel expenses.

Discrimination

The concerns regarding an outdated online assessment if proven to be truthful would have indirectly disadvantaged candidates with a disability when compared to those candidates who had no such challenges. Your former colleague may have also had a case of being denied a permanent employment opportunity given their perception of the moderators using the event to execute their revenge and having no prior training for the recruitment responsibility undertaken.

Race Discrimination

With regards to whether direct race discrimination has occurred in relation to the way that you were treated, it is useful to reflect upon the treatment that you and your former line manager received at the hands of the new line manager. The comparison shows similarities in treatment in that you were both perceived as a threat to be discarded by the manager and to this effect, you were treated no less favourably than the other manager. It is important to add that the law recognises that where a manager is a complete shite to everyone they work with, it does not make their behaviour discriminatory, only a complete shite and therefore equal treatment prevails.

However, you are the only person in the department with a different skin colour to your colleagues. Your former line manager shares the same skin colour as the new manager and your other colleagues. In addition to the issues outlined above, it cannot be ignored that after expressing concerns about the recruitment process, the manager assumed that your concerns related to race discrimination. The impact assessment report focused on race and none of the other protected characteristic, and all other accusations levied against you were race related.

It is noted that it is your manager, and not you, who has given attention to this specific issue and if it was not for your skin colour, would the issue of race have factored at all. The final insults were the deeply offensive verbal accusations and physical acts of segregation which became the final nail in the coffin of the catalogue of abusive and toxic behaviours. Bad manager or not, racism is racism and your work colleagues by their own behaviours, knowingly aided in the prohibited conduct. If you all shared the same skin colour, the conduct of the manager abusing their delegated authority would warrant the enactment of the formal disciplinary process, given the significant breaches to the trust and other terms of their employment contract with the organisation.

4 – Internal Recruitment Activity

Having worked since leaving secondary school and completing a part time business studies course, you begin a new job as an assistant secretary for a global organisation. Within a few weeks in the role, however, you find yourself twiddling your fingers as the secretary is reluctant to delegate any tasks beyond the recording of the executives' expenses. It is suggested that you provide support to the sales department who are experiencing an increase in workload, to which you agree.

The sales department consists of a dark skin male sales director, and two dark skin mature females who have occupied the sales manager and sales officer roles for an extremely long time and both are due to retire in the coming months. From dealing with new and existing customers' quotations to finalising and processing sales orders, liaising with other departments to problem solve and to meet all customer requirements, you are fully trained by both employees to manage all the duties within the sales department. Within a few weeks your role in the organisation formally changes to that of a full-time sales officer, but your salary remains unchanged as the salary in the old role is slightly higher than that of the new.

After several months, change in the sales department occurs with the departure of the manager, officer and the director who is quickly replaced with a young dark skin director. You work well together but customer demands results in the former manager being coaxed out of retirement to assist with the new orders, although this arrangement is short lived.

The new director decides to bring a mature dark skin female and former associate into the department to help clear the backlog until the manager position is filled. However, you find yourself having to train the support which defeated the objective of having a helping hand, but eventually things start to balance out. Finally, the manager position is advertised which both you and the support submit job application forms to the director, who later confirms that you both are the only two candidates in the competitive process.

A few days later, your sales colleague takes a sudden week's annual leave leaving you alone once again to manage the workload. One morning during their absence, you decide to take a coffee break and make a cuppa for the director as an excuse to obtain an update on the recruitment process. Placing the coffee cup on their desk, you ask the director about the interview arrangements only to be informed that the interview had taken place in the previous week and that the support had secured the sales manager position. You may have entered into a discussion about your application and lack of notification but all you recall is thinking that if ever there was a next time making them a cup of coffee, it would most definitely be a nice frothy cappuccino.

The relationship between you and the new sales manager remains cordial for a time but then you notice that your duties and responsibilities progressively increase to the point that you now perform most of the manager's duties whilst they spend their time chatting on the telephone. The increased duties also include the expectation that you drop everything to make the manager a drink whenever they command, which creates additional conflict between you.

Your complaints to the director about the additional burdens are met with promises to address the matter but nothing changes. In fact, the situation becomes worse to the point that your disagreements occur daily. Your staple response of your job description having no requirement to lubricate the manager on demand and politely suggesting they made their own drinks irritates them, but the manager expects you to do as you are told. Conversations with the director about the escalating problems serve no purpose and their promises are nothing but empty gestures to appease you.

Feeling that enough is enough, you decide to speak with the director to articulate a choice option to remedy the problems with the manager, either they or you leave the organisation. The director on hearing the options, makes their preference clear and so you submit a written notice and depart the organisation the following week.

A few months later, you attend the wedding reception of a former finance colleague and learn from your ex-colleagues in attendance that the sales director and manager were no longer employed at the organisation. Their departure was due to a catalogue of errors which had cost the business significantly with the loss of its customers and so the retirees had been asked once again to return to the now failing local organisation.

The Recruitment

Best practices are always advocated when carrying out internal and external recruitment drives. Acknowledging candidate applications and responding to general enquiries to providing feedback when requested is just fundamental good recruitment practice. Where recruitment processes are not transparent then candidate may view the methods adopted as unfair.

Misconduct

When an employee raises a concern or a complaint with their manager regarding a problem with work or a colleague, it is reasonable for the manager to attempt to resolve the matter informally and provide the employee with feedback. Where problems persist, then initiating the organisation's formal process such as a disciplinary action would not be unreasonable to ensure that lessons are learnt and not repeated.

It is noted that you did not raise a formal grievance about the behaviour of the manager, as this action may have resulted in a satisfactory outcome to your complaints. It is further noted that you were not guided by the director towards this course of action, as one would expect from a reasonable manager seeking to resolve a problem that cannot be dealt with informally.

Irrespective of how many times you complained to the director about the conduct of the manager, no action was taken to rectify the problem, whether with an informal chat, mediation, or the initiation of formal action. The director's inaction to the problem that was brought to their attention can only be interpreted as their belief that no problem existed. As a result, this inaction gave approval of the manager's continued mistreatment and hostility towards you and therefore those of the organisation, of whom the director is an employee and senior representative. Given that the actions of the director and the manager influenced your departure from the organisation, it would be difficult for the organisation to evidence that their behaviours and actions were not intentional.

Discrimination

It is possible that the sales director did not see you as a suitable candidate for the sales manager role because of your age. The director may have assumed that you lacked the knowledge and experience for such a responsible position which is why your application form met its untimely demise in the paper shredder under his desk. However, your former employment experience, qualifications and having to train the manager, would make any attempt to defend this viewpoint weak.

The unreasonable and demeaning treatment including that of the cups of tea harassment goes beyond any reasonable management instructions. It is not possible to know whether another employee would have experienced the same treatment if they shared the same skin colour as the director and manager.

But what is clear is that the conduct resulting in the slave like conditions of the additional imposed manager's duties, the expected adherence to all management demands without challenge or additional pay, and the lack of constructive action or support by the director, all indicate that the mistreatment was because of your skin colour.

5 – Promotion Opportunities

Working in a small team, you are one of two white skin employees operating in low pay grades within the department, with you operating as an adviser and the other as the assistant. Within weeks, your team leader recognises your capabilities and provides you with additional duties which align to those responsibilities carried out by the junior manager. You and the junior manager are now line managed by the team leader although there is no change to your pay or grade. Your department sits within a building occupied by the headquarters and so you have easy access to and enjoy friendships with a variety of people working within the organisation.

Each morning you find yourself speaking to a dark skin man who wears the most dapper of designer suits whenever you see him in the lifts before reaching your department. Your conversations are light-hearted and comical with you either voicing approval or disgust at the chosen tie worn with the dapper designer suit of the day. It does not occur to you that neither of you know the other's name, but you know that he works somewhere within the head office.

Following the Monday morning ritual with Mr dapper suit man, you greet your colleagues and make the usual round of

217

drinks before starting the day's work. The senior manager who heads the department enters the kitchen and asks that you to see to a director visiting the office for a meeting and to serve them drinks on their arrival. At the appointed time, you open the door to find Mr dapper suit man. Both shocked at seeing each other, you formally introduce yourself and share another joke whilst entering the senior manager's office. You serve drinks before returning to your desk to work.

The following day, you arrive at the office with the usual greetings and ritual of drink making before starting your day. You enter the senior manager's office to check whether they wanted a drink, but they appear to be engrossed reading a letter that you receive no reply to your offer and so you leave them in peace. The next day and same ritual, once again the senior manager does not respond to your offer of a drink and this time, they are looking out the window, but you do not take their unresponsiveness to heart. On the third time of being ignored, you stop the routine of including the manager in your drinks round. You begin to think that they were probably having a few off days, possibly week, possibly it was that time of the month.

As the workdays blend into weeks, the unresponsiveness extends beyond your tea making offers to them refusing to make any eye contact or to engage with you in any work matter. Your greetings are met with silence or a look in a different direction whenever you cross paths on a corridor or in other departments. To them you no longer existed. The only time that your senior manager will speak to you is when responding to a direct work-related question requiring their consent or action.

You do not take it to heart, especially when other colleagues notice their behaviour towards you and want to know what is going on. You cannot answer because you have no idea. You also notice that one of the directors whose office you would pop into for the occasional natter, had also began giving you the cold shoulder treatment. This does not surprise you too much as it was well known in the organisation that most of the appointed directors were a close-knit circle of former university students who had been 'handed' their positions by their boss. Thankfully, the continued relationship with your colleagues and team leader remains positive that you can continue your work without hinderance.

Change occurs in the office with several of your colleagues including the assistant, leaving because of secondments or promotion opportunities. With the junior manager post becoming vacant, you decide to apply for the role given that you had been carrying out the duties for a long time now. Your performance appraisals, whilst always extremely positive, did not provide the equivalent pay to that of the junior manager's post. You are temporarily promoted and receive an enhancement in your pay for an interim period whilst the role is advertised. Although having the qualification and the practical experience of line manging the admin and temporary workers in the department, you still attend training courses to ensure that all bases are covered in preparation for the interview.

The interview begins and progresses well with you answering all the questions, leaving the panel members in no doubt that you were a serious contender for the role. Then with the final question the chairperson asks a finance related question based on the reported activity in a particular financial broadsheet newspaper. Surprised by the unexpected question, you respond as best as possible whilst scanning your brain for possible answers. You recall that the job description did not specify the requirement for stock trading analytical skills, only the authorising of minor travel expenses. The chairperson decides to shoot another obscure financial question at you that prompts your arms to do vogue movements in the air. Instinctively, you know that by the end of the interview the job would be offered

220

elsewhere, which is proven correct. The successful candidate who is also your new line manager, has no experience in the specialism or in line managing people that your former line manager asks that you to train them.

After a few months, the new junior manager takes a holiday abroad but decides not to return to the office, preferring instead to take a long-term sick break before eventually resigning the role. Once again you are temporarily promoted but history repeats itself when the role is advertised. On this occasion however, no one is appointed and so your temporary promotion continues until the role is re-advertised. Third time being the charm, you endure another interview ritual to finally discover that the original junior manager has secured the job and returns to the office. You do not mind so much because there would be no requirement for you to train them to do the job.

Your team leader informs you that the junior manager will now line manage you which triggers the beginning a beautiful relationship. The manager, quite rightly, expects you to perform the duties of an advisor and not those of a junior manager. Honeymoon over, you find yourself occasionally clashing with your new line manager due to differences in operational opinions. One such occasion leads to a heated exchange where you are told in no uncertain terms that '*Your job is not to think but to do as you are told*'. On being put in your place, you acknowledge the instruction and promise to honour the duties specified in your job description moving forward.

The following day, you arrive to work on time and carry out the administrative duties. Receiving and recording queries which are forwarded to colleagues for action, in addition to typing letters and franking the post. When your manager asks you to produce a letter, you clarify that your duties were restricted to the typing and not the compilation of correspondence. In the following days, a backlog of work begins to form and so the team leader decides to resume their line responsibility of you, enabling your return to 'normal duties' on an advisor's salary. The junior manager continues their role for a few more months before obtaining promotion externally.

History repeats with the temporary promotion, the role advertisement, the interview ritual, and the appointment of someone else into the role of junior manager in the department. This time, the new line manager is the admin worker you once line managed on joining the organisation. Although disappointed with the outcome of the interview, you are pleased that a fellow

222

white skin co-worker had achieved promotion into a management position.

The opportunity to explore other avenues occurs with a secondment in the head office's finance department. Although led by the chairperson of your many failed interviews, you felt the time was right to move on, at least you will no longer be a ghostly white walker figure to your senior manager. Surprisingly you enjoy working with your new dark skin colleagues in the finance department and discover that the director has a dry sense of humour. You become impressed at your ability to touch type on a number pad as well as the QWERTY keyboard and produce an updated new starter induction pack with guidance on conducting batch and pay runs.

After a while in the role, your new line manager informs you of a new junior manager vacancy within another location of the organisation, but your former interview experiences make you reluctant to apply for the role. Anyway, your new focus is deciding on whether to study the ACCA or the AAT accountancy qualification.

Summoned to the director's office the following morning, you are told in no uncertain terms to apply for the junior manager's position as the director did not want you to do yourself a disservice. Their persuasion leads you to commit to applying for the role one last time. When invited to attend an interview, you purchase a finance broad sheet to read on your journey, just in case. The day goes well, with the interview panel asking questions relevant to the role and your former experiences and within days you are offered the job.

Informing the director of your good news and thanking them for their support, you hear an apology escape from their lips. Seeing your surprised expression, the director explains that they had been misinformed by your former senior manager about your character which had influenced the former interview outcomes. They had been given explicit instructions to deny you any promotion opportunities but having discovered your true character, they realised that the senior manager's actions had been so malicious that they felt compelled to rectify their wrongdoing. Pleased to have another fresh start and this time with some distance between you and the former senior manager, you happily forgive the director and go along your merry little way.

Joining the new team, you quickly settle into your new role and whilst you find yourself the only white skin person in the department, your new colleagues are extremely supportive and friendly. While having an informal chat with your new line manager, they tell you of a series of telephone calls from your former senior manager. They had been persistent with their guidance against your selection for interview and subsequent appointment into the junior manager's post. You learn that each call was aimed to demolish your character and by the time of their final call, your new manager was told '*You will regret ever having hired her because she will make your life a living hell*'.

Senior Manager's Behaviour

The role of management operating at any level within the organisation is to uphold the values and the established rules which are expressed within the organisation's policies and contract of employment. Senior managers hold a higher level of expected conduct, integrity and professionalism which is reflected in their status, pay and areas of accountability. Lead by example is the unspoken mantra by which senior managers showcase these expected leadership qualities aimed to infuse respectful inclusivity within the workplace.

The reason for the senior manager's conduct towards you is unknown although some may attribute their behaviour to a psychotic condition for which medical specialists have yet to find a cure. It seems coincidental that your white walker metamorphosis occurred following the observed interaction with the director when visiting your department. It may be that the senior manager considered your banter with the director to be somewhat inappropriate and possibly jumped to a conclusion that you had become their office garden tool. (Yeah, I know what you were thinking!!). In such instances it would have been reasonable for the senior manager to resolve their concerns with an informal chat. But they did not, and you continued to enjoy your friendship with Mr dapper suit man.

Discrimination

It is acknowledged that anything done by a person in the course of their employment will be treated as being done by the employer. The organisation therefore becomes liable for the conduct of its employees, including those that operate within the senior levels of the structure. There is also the expectation that management adheres to the discrimination law and not to unfairly treat an employee in the opportunities to access promotion.

Learning that the senior manager maliciously influenced your attempts of achieving promotion to the junior manager position on numerous occasions, would support a claim of less favourable treatment. Conducting the duties of a junior manager for a lengthy period and on occasions without the recognised pay, even training a new appointee into the position, would counter any claims of your unsuitability for the position. Furthermore, the same position secured in a different location confirmed your suitability. The conduct of the senior manager that are known to you, fully support the legal definition of discrimination and harassment.

The behaviour of the senior manager towards other members of staff must be given due consideration as it is possible that your former colleagues were treated just as poorly by the senior manager. Whether or not this is the case, the fact remains that the significant difference between you and your former senior manager is one of skin colour, which makes their actions racially motivated. The appointment of the white skin assistant to the junior manager's position does not negate the malicious intentions shown towards you and how you were made to feel by the conduct. Racism is racism and no mental disorder, ignorance or Basil Fawlty management style absolves the senior manager of their actions just because they hate you more than they hate the new junior manager.

Finally, it should be noted that whether you share a skin colour or not with the senior manager, their conduct of abusing their delegated authority and the organisation's trust and values, is such that the enactment of the formal disciplinary process is warranted. The significant breaches to their employment contract and equality law makes this a case for a zero-tolerance enforcement.

6 - Performance Appraisal

Your performance review meeting with your dark skin line manger confirms the achievement of the mutually agreed challenging objectives and projects. These achievements exceeded your manager's expectation of just maintaining local and national key performance indicators. In recognition of your achievement, the manager informs you of their intention to award the highest performance appraisal rating, which pleases you. Knowing that this decision would require the feedback and sign off from the dark skin regional manager, you were in no doubt that your line manager's recommendation would be supported. Within days of the meeting, however, you suddenly experience a back strain that places you on sick leave for two weeks.

During the first week of your absence from work, a few of your colleagues visit bearing gifts and to check on your recovery, which you appreciate. They mention a request by the regional manager to visit with you the following day to discuss a work matter. You let them know that the proposed visit would clash with your GP appointment and ask that the regional manager awaits your return to the office.

The following morning whilst slowly walking up the road to your GP appointment, a sports car stops alongside you and on turning, you see the regional manager in the driver's seat. After preliminary greetings, the regional manager offers you a lift to your appointment which you politely decline, explaining that the low baring car would undo your progress and walking helped to ease the stiffness in your back. They mention wanting to have a conversation, but you again suggest that they await your return to the office, to which they mumble a response before speeding off as if to chase Lewis Hamilton's crown.

As you begin to feel better towards the end of the second week, you notice a hand delivered A4 envelope in your post box. Opening the envelope, you find your performance appraisal form which is now completed by both the line and regional managers. Turning to the last page of the document to read your regional manager's comments, you suddenly feel your back begin to seize up again. The regional manager has downgraded the recommended performance rating by your line manager. Their rating indicated that your performance throughout the year, had merely met the fundamentals of the role. The justification for the downgrade was explained as follows:

- The achievements were part of the role duties, and the score was not justified.

- You had failed to complete the contracted workdays due to the back strain.

- You had failed to provide prior notice of the sick absence, which was deemed unauthorised and would remain unpaid.

- Formal action (disciplinary) would be taken for what was viewed as a serious act of misconduct.

A meeting to discuss the comments on your return to work is proposed and so you take your time, the weekend, to record an appropriate response to the regional manager's comments. You do not add your signature to the report to demonstrate your objections to the decision and hope that it would signal HR's intervention. Reviewing the company policies and recalling the absences of other colleagues to use as comparators, you compile a series of questions to challenge the regional manager's decision on your return to work.

Attending a meeting with the regional manager, you question their decision and thought process whilst taking notes but irrespective of your evidence to counter their assertions, the regional manager remains inflexible and refuses to alter their

231

comments. The meeting ends with you advising them of your intention to pursue the matter further.

On seeking initial advice from the HR department, you raise a formal grievance which is sent to the service director and copied to the HR manager. Several days later, the HR manager calls you into their office and informs you that an outcome to your grievance has been reached. The original appraisal box rating given by the line manager would hold precedence given that they and not the regional manager was best placed to evaluate the objectives achieved. HR also confirmed that no formal action would be taken against you for being ill and confirmed that you would be paid for the period of absence in accordance with the company's policy. When enquiring about the regional manager's unreasonable conduct, you are asked to trust HR that the situation would be managed. You receive no further communication from HR thereby allowing the regional manager to continue their reign.

Performance Appraisals

Appraisals form part of the performance management systems that the organisation will have in place to measure performance and reward employees for work well done. The cycle begins at the start of the reporting year when mutually agreed objectives are set for achieving and are periodically reviewed by you and your line manager. These review meetings provide the opportunity to adjust or to add new objectives where initial targets have been achieved. Throughout this period and especially at the final review meeting, the manager will provide an indication of the award mark to expect so that there are no surprises when the reporting year reaches an end.

The aim of this process is to build on skills and not merely to demonstrate the ability to carry out the work that an employee is hired to perform. Where performance problems persist however, the formal route of a performance improvement plan may be initiated. Any sick absences that occur throughout the reporting year may impact upon the set objectives, but line managers are expected to be reasonable by adapting or extending targets to accommodate for these incidents, hence the reason for objectives being SMART.

Senior Manager's Behaviour

Whilst the situation was remedied to your financial satisfaction, the issue of unfair treatment remains. It is possible that the senior manager genuinely believed you had not achieved your appraisal objectives. A reasonable person would have spoken with the line manager to review and even debate the evidence of your achievement before expressing their views on the report. You presume this event did occur, but the senior manager had already formed their opinion and attempted to take advantage of your sick absence to progress their agenda. HR confirmed that you had correctly followed the organisation's policy when reporting your ill health, so what would cause the senior manager to deny you the performance reward and want to pursue formal action against you?

Discrimination

The application of fair treatment towards employees remains the same as in the previous example, that is, for managers not to discriminate against an employee by denying them access to receiving benefits of the organisation, such as that awarded through the performance appraisal system. Being in a position of seniority and empowered to ensure the effective operation of the department and its employees does not give permissions to threaten and misuse company rules to serve a personal agenda. The regional manager's attempts to initiate formal action using two further organisational policies appear to serve the purpose of deterring your career progression and diminishing your accomplishments. Especially as performance appraisals formed part of the organisation's consideration

234

process of future job promotions. By asserting their control over you, the regional manager would be able to suppress all attempts that you made to develop and to progress in your career.

Had the regional manager's intentions been successful, your hard work and long hours throughout the appraisal year would have been recorded as fulfilling the duties of the job. In turn, this would mean the establishment of a new and much higher performance standard and benchmark that you would be expected to maintain and be measured against, when carrying out your everyday duties.

The two weeks sick leave would have gone unpaid, and you would have been sanctioned even possibly dismissed because of the perceived serious/gross misconduct of taking sick leave. Punishment, intensified workload, and longer hours for a meagre pay, sounds fair?

However, consideration must be given to whether you would have been treated any differently if you had shared the same skin colour as your colleagues. Given that you were the only person to receive such treatment, then the reason can only be because of your skin colour. Especially when you consider the attempt to abuse the organisational policies to deny you sick pay and impose a misconduct sanction, possibly to achieve a dismissal. This conduct show that on the balance of probability, the senior manager's actions were maliciously intended. Based on this reasoning, the conduct of the senior manager abusing their authority and the organisation's trust and values, warrants the enactment of the formal disciplinary process. The significant breaches to their employment contract and equality law, makes this a case for zero tolerance policy enforcement.

7 – 360 Performance Management

Years in a customer facing role leaves you no longer motivated and so you decide upon a change of pace and secure a secondment position. Your technical skills and knowledge would be better utilised in the new role and although not a mobile role, the duties require you to interact with local and national employees.

The new department suffers from a high turnover of line and senior managers, none of whom are in post long enough to discuss your objectives and the accredited technical training required by all post holders. However, as the secondment term approaches its end, new department managers are appointed who extend your secondment for an indefinite period, to your satisfaction.

In the first meeting with your new dark skin line manager, you discuss and agree objectives and the accredited technical training course. You agree to provide details about the course at your next review meeting, and on checking with your colleagues and the HR department, you learn that the organisation's development programme sourced the required training course.

In your next review meeting, the new dark skin senior manager joins your line manager which gives you the opportunity to finally meet them, although you find their presence unusual and contrary to general practice. The meeting goes well, and you are asked to complete the necessary training documents for your manager to approve, which you action once the meeting has ended. On discussing the training course at the next review meeting, your line manager informs you that the search for an external training provider and the associated cost, were your responsibility and not those of the organisation. Having already checked the information, you felt it best to recheck before responding and following the meeting you again receive confirmation that the organisation funded the accredited course through a preferred supplier. You email the details to your line manager who responds that they now wanted to check for themself and would provide an update at the next scheduled meeting.

Once again, the senior manager finds themself in your review meeting as both managers want to discuss your objectives. The meeting begins well until the senior manager makes a comment about your communication style. You mention that none of your current or former managers, team members or customers had ever expressed concerns about your communication style, in fact quite the opposite. You say that you always welcome the opportunity to improve upon skills that may be lacking and ask for examples of the problem. The senior manager tells you that they felt your communication style was not in line with the corporate standards and values and that you needed to reflect upon it. The meeting ends abruptly leaving you to wonder what on earth were they talking about.

The senior manager is again present at the next meeting and repeats their comments about your communication style but fails to elaborate. Having checked the organisation's values and expectations you convey your belief of having done nothing untoward, but the senior manager tells you that you must identify and address the problem. Que?

Finally, your manager provides an example at the next meeting. They had observed your recent interactions with team members earlier in the week, moving from desk to desk and speaking to them all, which they viewed as positive. In contrast, on the following day you had stayed at your desk with your head down and failed to interact with anyone. You immediately notice that the example is focused on a recent rather than any earlier events that prompted a cause for concern. Very patiently you explain that the first example was a necessity as you were resolving a problem that required you to access each team member's desktop whereas the second example reflected there being no technical problem to resolve which enabled you to catch up on yours and an absent colleague's workload. You continue to explain that these examples did not in any way evidence a communication problem neither did it demonstrate you being an anti-social animal but someone who values their job. You remind the managers that you had worked in the organisation for some years and knowing most of the workforce, have always been civil and polite in all your interactions with them.

However, the senior manager reiterates their concerns and announces that they will be conducting a 360-degree review to gain feedback from your colleagues. Concerned that this new development is both inappropriate and exposes you to the unfair critiquing of colleagues, you ask whether the new review is to be a standardised practice for the team. The senior manager tells you that they had no reason to extend the practice to everyone as it was personal to you. Whilst they recognised their decision to be irregular, they knew that 360s were carried out for lots of reason.

Now standing on their parapet, the senior manager continues their sermon by telling you that the feedback would provide the opportunity to see the responses before taking a good look at yourself. You will then be able to decide what changes you could make within yourself because it is for you to take the action. They could not make you change and communicate more, and they could not make you do anything because they were your behaviours. It is for you to decide whether you want to align to the organisation's values and communicate a bit more with the team. It is completely up to you. Wow!!

Aware that the organisation did not conduct 360 performance reviews as a standard practice and concerned at the tone of the senior manager's insistence of a communication problem, you decide to speak to the HRBP assigned to your department about the meetings. You articulate your concerns of how this newly imposed and targeted process would reflect negatively on your work relationships. However, the HRBP begins to regurgitate the sermon of the senior manager most high, leaving you in no doubt that gaining any constructive support would be futile.

The senior manager informs you at the next meeting, that the 360 reviews were almost completed and would be forwarded to you. Both the managers raise another issue about your communication style. This time, your manager mentions you

241

not making the effort to speak to the new recruits who had visited the team earlier in the week and you had remained at your desk. By now you are annoyed with the nonsense but patiently explain that you were not aware of any new recruits visiting the office. As an open planned floor space that contains several other business functions, it was not unusual to see new faces on the floor walking around. Whilst you noticed a couple of new faces talking to one or two of your colleagues, you had not been made aware that they were new starters for the department. Furthermore, you stress that neither of the managers had notified the team about the planned visit either verbally or by email and had made no effort to introduce the visitors to each of the team members on their arrival. That said, you explain having already communicated with several of the new recruits when setting them up on the system and dealing with technical queries. You then question how the example demonstrated a failure on your part to meet the corporate values. The senior manager responds by telling you '*It is up to you to identify and correct your own behaviour.*'

Later in the day you receive copies of the completed 360-degree performance reviews by your team members and notice that none of feedback references communication as a problem.

In fact, most comments are extremely positive and the only 'negative' relates to an incomplete task, which due to a colleague's absence you took the initiative to remedy days earlier.

A virus, fortunately not Covid, makes its round throughout the office and finally reaches you towards the end of the week. Struggling to contain the sniffles and coughs, you despatch an email to your line manager and copy the senior manager into the communication. You inform them of your ill health and imminent departure from the office once a task is completed.

At the start of the new working week, you notice an email from your line manager questioning why you had failed to inform them of your sick absence. You refer them to the communication despatched in the previous week and confirmed that you had followed the company's policy. However, your line manager responds by instructing you to notify all your team members of any sick absences that you have in the future. In response, you 'remind' the line manager that such instruction was contrary to both sickness and data protection policies due to their highly personal and confidential nature.

Your line manager is alone at your next review meeting which provides you with the opportunity to ~~let rip~~ explain your views of the bullying behaviour received and the senior managers' unreasonable expectations and unfair treatment. You express serious concern that their actions and comments had abused the organisation's values and policies. On hearing your concerns, the line manager acknowledges how their actions may have been perceived as unfair and promises to discuss the matter with the senior manager.

You encounter no further problems from both managers and the senior manager stops attending your review meetings. The approval of your technical training course, unfortunately, remains outstanding.

Secondments

Secondments are an opportunity to develop and expand an employee's skills by working in a different role and department for a given period. These may take place within the organisation or with a client organisation and are beneficial for; mitigating redundancy risk with a temporary redeployment option, developing workforce talent especially in succession planning or performance improvements, or as a gap filler until a vacant position is filled. Regular meetings occur between the line manager and seconded employee to discuss development plans and progress which is not dissimilar to those of performance appraisal reviews. When providing feedback, line managers are expected to provide clear advice and evidence to support the employee in their development, including the provision of any appropriate training for upskilling.

Technical Training Course

The accredited technical training was confirmed as a requirement of your seconded role and was provided as part of the organisation's staff development package. The procrastination and subsequent failure by your managers to provide their consent for this development need was unfair. By not affording an employee access to training or any other benefits that it provides to other employees then the organisation is deemed to have discriminated if the difference in treatment is because of a protected characteristic.

The 360 Appraisal Review

Many organisational policies are collectively agreed through negotiations between the employer and trade union organisations and or employee representatives. This is to ensure the fairness and consistent application of the organisational rules to the entire workforce. All key policies and processes are contained in the staff handbook and are an expressed term in the employee's contract of employment. As such, the introduction

245

of any new processes or procedures that alters the terms of the existing arrangement must first have the unions and or employee representative consent after members have been consulted. Without this process, the organisation will be viewed as unilaterally imposing new rules and possibly breaching its contractual agreement with its employees. The decision of your managers to conduct a new performance review process without just cause and was not equally applied to all employees, will be viewed as unfair.

Communication Style

Communication styles, encompasses many different methods and when a manager expresses concern about your communication style, you automatically assume the worst of having said or written something inappropriate that may have caused offence to someone. Requesting details of the alleged concern is not unreasonable, however, after significant delays, the examples provided by the managers had the common theme that focused on your physical interaction with people.

Management Behaviours

All managers are expected to have a clear understanding of the organisations' rules and standards and to have experience of managing a team or resources. Whilst managing a team has its challenges, the services of human resources are available to provide both managers and employees with constructive support and guidance to maintain a harmonious working environment.

When the senior manager first expressed their concern about your communication style, they failed to supply the evidence. When the examples were provided, they implied a lack of sufficient physical engagement with your colleagues. The level of interaction appeared to have been measured by the number of times you got up from your desk to speak with people. This implied that the managers held an unreasonable expectation that went beyond your duties to satisfy their subjective view of the organisation's communication values. Given that your role largely dealt with system improvements and technical problem-solving on a national and local level, engagement would have been easily measurable without your need to physically move from a desk. More importantly, the role did not require you to engage in needless chatter to satisfy your managers' concerns. The use of the organisation's values as a weapon combined with an unused assessment method on one employee and not all, is unethical and unfair. It is noted that the managers' actions were supported with approval from the HRBP, who ignored your concern.

247

Discrimination

Where a manager or employee treats another employee less favourably during their employment, the treatment is viewed as being carried out by the organisation. There is the expectation that management adheres to the Equality law and not discriminate against an employee in the way that they are afforded access to opportunities such as training and development.

The denied technical training course, the insistence of a communication problem and pursuant of an unapproved performance review process, are all evidence of unfair treatment. The continual presence of the senior manager at your review meetings may be viewed as intimidation, given that their actions was not in accordance with standard organisational practice.

It is the sermon by the senior manager that is most detrimental because it transforms the alleged performance concern into a personal attack. The insistence that you look at yourself and your behaviour to rectify the perceived problem from within, simply infers that you are the problem. Engagement with your colleagues could have been measured through a variety of methods such as surveys and dashboard monitoring.

248

Record keeping of moving one's posterior from one's chair to speak with colleagues is not a familiar performance monitoring technique, unlike electronic and telecommunication usage. The subjective actions and behaviours of the managers were not applied to any other person, and so the difference in treatment that you received can only infer a reason of skin colour.

Irrespective of you having a protected characteristic or not, the conduct of all the managers abusing their delegated authority and the organisation's rules and values, warrants the enactment of the formal disciplinary process. The significant breaches to their employment contracts make this a zero-tolerance policy matter.

8 - Sick Leave Allegation

Managing a small team who provide specialist support to various departments in an organisation, for once, you are not the only white skin person in the department. There are two other employees who share your skin colour, but they are of different ethnicities, with one working full time and the other part time. Both are members of your team alongside a dark skin employee.

Having former experience of managing a team, you find that this time around, the white full-time team member constantly poses a challenge for the team with their annoying behaviours. Known for being a drama queen, the full timer will often over analyse or over complicate the most simplistic of tasks. You have learnt that it is their coping mechanism to hide their inability to perform to a reasonable standard. Suffering from an inflated ego that needs medical attention, the full timer informs anyone who cares to listen of their intention to pursue a new career path as the current post was not fulfilling their ambitions. Yet they also have a habit of speaking with dark skin managers whenever you delegate or provide them guidance on a task. Whilst preferring not to view their actions as an attempt to undermine your abilities, you ignore this activity as you know they had applied for your job and probably still felt aggrieved at

250

your success. Irrespective of their feelings, your peers and senior colleagues in the organisation constantly acknowledge your competence and praise your management capabilities.

An excessive amount of your time is spent stroking the ego of the full timer to encourage them to work while the other team members just get on with it. Whether upset by the harsh words from a department manager due to an incomplete task or whether it is the breakup of yet another relationship, you are always sympathetic and supportive. These upsets usually trigger a period of sick or annual leave which provides the remaining team members with the opportunity to resolve errors before the full timer's return to work.

Unfortunately, as soon as the full timer settles back into work, their antics become even more annoying creating increased levels of complaints that it now raises serious competency issues. Your attempts to encourage improvements have failed which means there is now no escaping the initiation of a formal improvement plan. Previous discussions with your line manager on the topic have resulted in procrastination because they are acutely aware of the full timer's volatile temperament. However, before any plans can be put into action, the full timer takes another period of sick leave citing a virus for

251

the reason. Following the company's absence policy and procedures, you maintain contact with the full timer and ensure that certificates covering their absence are logged on receipt. Any discussions about work activities are restricted to general issues during the keep in touch communications, as your priority is to ensure that they recover from their ailment. They let you know that a series of tests found nothing to diagnose and so they were pursuing alternative remedies to resolve their condition.

With a team member absent from the office, you notice that the remaining members are more productive, in fact the whole department seemed more hyper than usual. You put this down to the sun streaming through the office windows, but the atmosphere is so positive that you could swear that you heard someone organising a ~~carnival~~, garden fete.

On receipt of the full timer's latest sick certificate, you notice a change in the reason for the absence from to the usual '*Iliedtogetsometimeoffworkitus*' to a neurological disorder. You contact HR to discuss the sudden change and they agree to your suggestion of a referral to occupational health to obtain some practical guidance for supporting the full timer's return to the office.

Having the responsibility for booking the appointment, you must first speak with the full timer but on picking up the phone to make the call, you suddenly hesitate before hanging up. You have no reason to feel uncomfortable, but you do, and the alarm bells refuse to stop ringing in your head, getting louder as you pick up the phone again to dial their number. You try to reason that you are just being silly because logic tells you that the cause of their ailment had nothing to do with work and yet the uncomfortable feeling you have will not subside.

Your chat with the full timer begins well and you notice that they are unusually chirpy which you guess is their new medication taking effect. You learn that they expect to return to work within a couple of weeks which you note will nicely avoid the triggering of their reduced pay. The recommended referral to occupational health is agreed with the full timer. They continue to let you know that they had learnt through alternative support activities that their working relationship with you and the way you line managed them had been the cause of their ill health. They had previously felt unable to talk with you about these concerns because they felt you kept putting them down to the extent that they would '*rather go to anyone else than you.*' The statement is repeated several times as if to stress a point. They

253

then tell you that they felt relieved to have expressed their concern and were now looking forward to a '*better working relationship with you*' before terminating the call.

Stunned by this development, you hear yourself say '*What the f**k?!!*' Reflecting on the relationship, you know that you had been very supportive and may have treated them more favourably than other team members because their personality demanded it. You thought that accommodating their behaviour helped to maintain an effective functioning team. You strongly doubted that your management style was the cause of their illness but felt a conversation with HR services was needed.

The dark skin HR Business Partner (HRBP) tells you not to worry and that it was likely that the full timer was looking for someone to blame for their problems. They tell you their reaction was natural and part of the recovery process, which does not make you feel any better. The HRBP, who proudly tells you that they have thirty years' experience and knows what they are talking about, tries to assure you that the occupational health report would resolve matters. However, on receipt of the report you see the handwritten additional comments made by the full timer on the report, clearly reiterating that you were the cause of their illness.

254

You receive an email from the HRBP inviting you to a pre-meeting to discuss the full timer's return to work plans, but after expressing that it would not be sensible for you to conduct the meeting given the allegation, you are made to attend anyway. You reiterate your concerns in the pre-meeting only to be met with the 30 years of experience and the *'It's your responsibility as the line manager'* comments but you stand your ground. You insist that either yours or another manager conducts the return-to-work meeting, to which the HRBP reluctantly agrees. You stress the importance of acquiring specific details of the allegation as it would assist in managing the identified issues going forward. You also suggest that the full timer is moved to another team or department whilst the perceived cause of their illness is properly investigated and to avoid any additional allegations. However, when the full timer returns to work, your line manager conducts the meeting with the HRBP with 30 years' experience and neither raises the allegation made against you. So, the full timer returns to your team as if butter wouldn't melt.

Surprised that your suggestions were disregarded, you are left to continue managing the full timer without any feedback provided from the meeting. This poses a challenge as you begin to second guess your decisions and instructions to the team, suspicious that the full timer will be ready to pounce at any wrong move.

Reflecting upon the reasons for the allegation which HR had ignored, you recall receiving no complaints about your management style from the team, your managers, or other colleagues in the organisation. Had there been a problem, then surely your manager would have discussed this with you in appraisals or a peer meeting alongside the praises for your achievements and problem-solving skills. The handwritten comments on an official report can only be viewed as a personal attack on your character and the allegation unless proven otherwise, will be deemed to be true. You view this as an attempt to discredit and to possibly have you dismissed so that the full timer could claim your crown. With reluctance, you decide to raise a grievance against the full timer citing discrimination because of the false and unsubstantiated allegation which you felt may be due to jealousy, but you also knew that your ethnicity was likely to have been an attributing factor, given their stated preference to go to other managers. You also request that a formal investigation is conducted given the serious concerns raised.

Your grievance is acknowledged, and an investigation meeting occurs a week later where the investigator is your dark skin senior manager who is supported by the HRBP with the 30 years' experience. You confirm in detail the efforts made to support the full timer in both work and with their personal issues and provide all evidence to corroborate your statements and names of witnesses. You explain that having reflected on your own conduct managing the full timer, you were satisfied that you had done nothing to warrant the malicious allegation.

The investigator discusses the grievance process but suggests an informal approach is adopted to resolve the issues raised. You reject the suggestion explaining that the opportunity had been lost weeks ago at the full timer's return to work meeting or any follow-up meetings. You point out that the risk of their continuing to work with you should have been assessed at that time as well as the reason for the allegation made against you. The investigator's suggestion of mediation is also rejected with the explanation that you had yet to learn the nature of the allegation, which leaves you powerless to protect or defend yourself. You clarify that you were waiting for an explanation for the allegation, but in its absence, you had no choice but to presume that your ethnicity was the reason for the accusation.

257

You muster all your self-control to continue to work professionally with the full timer whilst they carry on with their antics. Eventually, you receive a letter about the investigation which concludes that an informal process had been followed and whilst evidence had been collated, they were not disclosed to you. The investigator believed that no racism had occurred but fails to provide details of how they had reached this conclusion. You are presented with the option of mediation or raising a formal complaint if you remained dissatisfied. An offer to discuss the report findings is also offered whilst in the meantime, the investigator would attempt to resolve matters with the full timer.

Once again, no explanation or the context of the allegation against you has been disclosed and so you have no idea of what you are being accused. The report also fails to provide any information of the evidence collated which makes you wonder if any investigation had taken place at all. And what on earth did they mean about resolving the issues with the full timer? Your concerns and the impact that the situation was having on you are being completely ignored with priority being given to the full timer. Taking a few days to consider the options, you decide to

258

accept the offer to discuss the report findings with the investigator.

At the arranged meeting with the investigator, the dark skin senior HRBP is in attendance. Once again, the focus of the discussion is on the full timer's health and wellbeing and not your grievance. Your repeated request for an explanation for the allegation goes unanswered except for it being a matter of confidentiality that prevents them from disclosing the reason to you. They try to assure you that the matter is being sorted but their actions to date has left you with no confidence in their abilities.

You feel the onset of a headache from banging your head against a brick wall but are determined to resolve the issue. You propose a resolution with the full timer making a written retraction of the allegation which would put to rest your grievance otherwise you would have no option but to continue the formal process. Yet before the meeting ends you are again asked to decide on your next course of action, as if they had not heard your earlier ultimatum. So, you reiterate your proposed solution in an email to both the investigator and the senior HRBP and hope that they will do the right thing and listen to you.

259

Busy with work, you realise that a couple of weeks had passed since your email and that you had yet to receive a response to your proposal, so you email the senior HRBP for an update. In fact, you send several reminders before you finally receive a response. You are informed that your grievance had been closed because you had chosen not to pursue the option of mediation and that you did not appeal the outcome of the investigation.

The Allegation

Every person has the right to natural justice. Where there is an allegation made against an employee, it is necessary for the employee to be provided with sufficient information about the claim so that they may defend themselves against it. Where no defence is presented then the allegation is deemed to be true.

The nature of the alleged misconduct, the specifics of what was done, when it was done, where it was done, is fundamental information that was not disclosed to you. The failure to provide this information denied you natural justice and the right to defend yourself therefore you were considered as having no rights which made this act unfair.

Sick Absence

The organisation's sick absence policy will align with the duty of care to maintain a work environment that is safe and without risk to employees, where it is reasonably practicable. The policy will provide guidance on the steps that should be taken from the reported first day of an employee's absence until their return to the workplace. Guidance provided by the employee's GP or the organisation's occupational health service should be considered when aiding the employee's return to work.

The full timer's handwritten statement on the occupational health report alleging that you were the cause of their illness, required investigation. The return-to-work meeting provided the opportunity for the manager to obtain clarification about the allegation so that appropriate action could be taken. Whether conducting a health risk assessment or an investigation into the allegation, following a formal policy would have aided the resolution of the matter. Both HR and the investigating senior manager appear to have found a possible informal solution to the problem but this too, as the affected party, was not disclosed to you. As such the false account of your character is held on the organisation's record which may subsequently become

261

detrimental to your future career pursuits. The absence of a due process infers a lack of impartiality on the part of the organisation and therefore unfair/less favourable treatment.

Grievance

An employee may use the organisation's grievance policy to bring attention to a problem that may relate to a work process or unfair treatment that requires a resolution. As with the disciplinary process, where raised concerns have not been resolved informally, a formal process may be pursued to ensure that a just solution is achieved. Appointing an impartial manager may be necessary depending on the nature of the complaint. They will be responsible for acquiring witness statements and any other evidence to establish the facts of the matter, which on the balance of probability will indicate whether the allegation is true or not.

The investigation report and any evidence collated must be provided to the parties so that a fair opportunity is given to respond to the allegation for natural justice to be achieved. Throughout the process, employees have the right to be accompanied by a trade union representative or a work companion and have the right to appeal against any decisions reached by the hearing panel. Where the organisation lacks the specialist knowledge or skill to respond to an allegation internally, then it would be reasonable to seek the support of an external specialist.

Once interviewed about your grievance, the investigating manager and HR failed to follow the organisation's fair process and regressed the serious concern to the informal stages of the policy without your consent. With no explanation for the allegation, you were denied the right to defend yourself against the false claim. The statement that your complaint was not an act of race discrimination without corroborating evidence showed a lack of objectivity. Your recommended solution of the full timer's written retraction of the allegation was ignored, and your case was closed by HR without any prior notification. All these actions show a lack of impartiality and therefore unfairness.

Mediation

Mediation is an informal process where disputing employees may reach a solution to their workplace problems with the assistance of an impartial representative skilled at problem solving. Such steps are taken by organisations where general misconduct occurs with disagreements, personality clashes or general misunderstandings amongst employees. Mediation is not the appropriate solution to all workplace

263

disputes and must be avoided where serious allegations of gross misconduct such as discrimination are raised. This problem-solving solution may only occur if both parties know details of the subject matter under discussion and are mutually willing to partake in the event. As such, closing your grievance because you refused to engage in mediation, may be viewed as both unreasonable and unfair.

Discrimination

The organisation has a duty not to treat one employee less favourably than another employee because of a protected characteristic and they must not be subjected to any detriment in the terms and conditions of their employment with the organisation. Anything done by the employee in the course of their employment, is treated as also being done by the organisation who will be held liable. Claims of ignorance or incompetence in the management of employees and the terms of their employment will not excuse or absolve the organisation of its legal responsibilities.

Exploration of the possible reasons for the allegation made against you is not answered by the organisation and your own self-reflection on your management style provided no answers except one. Had any evidence from a formal investigation found that you were responsible for the full timer's absence from work, then an appropriate sanction would have brought the matter to an end. Speculating on the possible reasons for the allegation made against you could be explained by prescribed medication causing a temporary lapse in judgement resulting in the full timer's allegation, which would have corroborated the views of the HRBP with 30 years' experience. Another reason could be one of jealously given that everyone knew that the full timer had applied for your job.

The fact that a reason was not provided possibly meant that none existed which in turn makes the full timer's allegation malicious. The investigator's perception that your complaint was not race discrimination and the complacent approach adopted with your grievance appear to support an unspoken view formed by the investigator and HR, that the problem was a mere disagreement between two colleagues. The fact that you both shared the same skin colour most likely influenced this perception. However, had an impartial investigation been conducted, they may have learnt of the ethnic differences of both parties and how one ethnic group traditionally perceives the other as inferior and subservient. This would have provided context to the discrimination claim raised and why you

265

considered the full timer's allegation to be malicious, especially given their preference to '*go to anyone else but you*' statements. Instead, the failings by the investigator and the HR business partners, even with the 30 years of experience, collectively evidences the less favourable treatment shown towards you.

Had you shared the same skin colour as the staff members managing your complaint, then it is likely that your grievance would have been managed differently and in line with the organisation's policy. That said, their failure to follow a due process free from manipulation to satisfy a biased outcome, is an abuse of their delegated authority and a breach of the terms and conditions of your contract with the organisation. Whether they were fully aware of the implications of their actions or not, the detriment cause to you is such that enactment of the zero-tolerance policy is warranted.

9 - Fixed Term Contract

As an interim worker, you begin a fixed term contract covering the maternity absence in a large organisation. You and another white skin contractor share a job that is expected to last six months within a department of permanent dark skin employees.

Your new dark skin line manager's role is temporary to cover a long-term sick absence of the permanent manager. They are efficient holding regular review meetings to discuss your objectives and any challenges experienced which they assist in resolving. Overall, the acting manager is pleased with your performance, confirming that your competences superseded the expected standards and approves the completion of your probation with further positive comments.

Towards the end of your contract, the acting manager informs you about another contract opportunity in the department which is expected to last 12 months and promises to inform you once the role is advertised. When notified, you apply and secure the role whilst your peer is given an extension to their contract.

During a review meeting in your new role, the acting manager announces the expected return of the permanent manager which means your acting manager would be returning to their substantive position. You are thanked for your efforts and encouraged to apply for an expected permanent post that is to become vacant within the department in the coming months.

You meet the dark skin substantive line manager in a review meeting and use the opportunity to express an interest in the anticipated vacancy within the department. The manager promises to keep you informed of developments once the recruitment plans are known. However, unlike the acting manager, the manager holds no further meetings with you and so your probation and appraisal reviews go unactioned, unlike the individual meetings held with the permanent team members.

As the months go by you find that the only way to communicate with your manager is either through emails or whenever you cross paths in a corridor. Other than the regular team meetings, there is little opportunity to speak with your manager about any concerns you may have. On seeing the manager by chance in the corridor, you enquire about the now vacant permanent position. You are told that nothing tangible had been agreed but once again, you will be informed as soon as they had information to relay. So, you focus on your work as it is a busy time for the department.

Whilst in a staff meeting a couple of weeks later, one of your colleagues asks the manager whether they had yet decided upon a preferred candidate for the permanent post. The manager confirms that they had and expected the new appointee, a dark skin former associate, to take up their position shortly. Disappointed with this discovery, you raise a formal grievance of race discrimination and breach of the fixed term regulations, given that you were denied the opportunity to apply for the permanent role. Raising the grievance coincides with the pending end of your fixed term contract where no final meeting has been arranged with the manager.

Although an investigation is conducted on the receipt of your grievance, you are only provided with two emails showing the ethnic profile of anonymised candidates who were selected for interviews. No record of your recommended witnesses or any other statement or records are provided to you. Throughout the hearing process you learn about the recruitment timeline and that the permanent vacancy had been advertised a week prior to your last discussion with the manager. As the recruiting manager, they had been instrumental in all stages of the recruitment process. Twelve people had applied for the role which had been advertised for two weeks rather than the usual four. Had

269

hundreds of candidates applied for the vacancy, you would have understood the need to reduce the vacancy timeline, but not for twelve applicants. An advert had been placed on the organisation's website and with a recruitment agency who had managed the candidates' applications. The candidates were diverse and after selecting eight for interview the successful candidate was confirmed as a dark skin former associate of the organisation.

Neither your grievance nor the appeal against the original panel's decision are upheld. The reasons provided were repetitive in that the organisation had no obligation to inform you directly of any vacancy advertised, as this information was accessible to all employees on the organisation's website. Additionally, both internal and external candidates of all ethnicities had applied for the role and so the organisation was satisfied that no discrimination and no breach of the fixed term contract had occurred. However, they recognised that improvements with the updates to policies and processes were necessary, but they were satisfied that these would be sorted in due course.

Fixed Term Employee Contracts

A fixed term employee must not be treated less favourably than a comparable permanent employee of the organisation. The Fixed Term Employee (Prevention of Less Favourable Treatment) Regulations 2002 puts in place the requirement to safeguard the fair treatment towards fixed term employees. The aim is to ensure that they are not subjected to any detriment or deliberate failures of opportunities in the areas of training, securing permanent employment, transfers, benefits, facilities, or services of the organisation. With regards to the employment opportunities, there is a right to be informed of vacancies where the fixed term employee has a reasonable chance of seeing it or is given reasonable notice by the organisation.

With regards to the ending of the contract, a fixed term employee must be treated no differently to a permanent employee and as such, ending of the fixed term contract must be processed in the same way as if making a permanent employee redundant. The decision not to renew the fixed term contract is seen as a dismissal from the contract under the Employment Rights Act 1996.

Compliance with this law means following a redundancy process which entails holding a meeting to discuss the reason for the contract ending, ideally prior to the start of the notice period. Allowing the fixed term employee, the right to appeal against the dismissal and exploring any suitable alternative employment opportunities in the organisation. This may include placing the employee on a redeployment list so that they are notified of suitable vacancies until such time that either another position is secured, or the contract comes to an end.

Management Behaviour

After expressing an interest in the vacant role in the department on several occasions, your line manager who is also the recruiting manager, fails to inform you about the vacancy once it is advertised. The manager also fails to conduct the regular review meeting when compared to the permanent employees in the department. This process would have provided you with the opportunity to discuss the role and any other vacancies occurring in the organisation.

Discrimination

The actions of a manager towards an employee in the course of their employment, is treated as also being done by the organisation, who will be held liable. Claims of ignorance in the understanding of an employee's employment arrangements or the incompetence in the management of the arrangement will not excuse or absolve the organisation of its legal responsibilities.

You had the opportunity to apply for the vacant position on the organisation's website for the limited period of two weeks, had you been informed of the position going live. Had the manager mentioned the vacancy during your last conversation, there would have been no reason to raise a grievance. The ethnicity of the candidates who applied and were selected for interview is completely irrelevant. Your grievance relates to the line manager's failures when executing the terms of your contract resulting in the less favourable treatment shown towards you.

Having proven your capability to perform to a high standard in the role for which you were praised by the acting manager in regular meetings, the manager's actions is one of avoidance and noncompliance to the terms of your contract. This conduct infers an intent to restrict your access to the permanent post as you may have been perceived as being a strong candidate and therefore a likely threat to the preferred candidate.

Acquiring the preferred candidate's application for the permanent position may also explain the line manager's decision to shorten the duration of the job advertisement to less than the standard four-week period. Whether or not the manager was aware of the implications of their actions, is irrelevant. The collective evidence shows that on a balance of probability, their less favourable treatment towards you when compared to the management of the permanent colleagues and in terms of the permanent job opportunity, was because of your different employment arrangements and your skin colour.

10 - Recognition

As a white skin manager, you join some of the working groups established for the restructures taking place in the organisation. Through your work, you notice that a key policy to meet a legal requirement of the service has yet to be implemented. You produce and submit a business case to a senior director for consideration, setting out the work which the organisation needed to act upon to become compliant. You become a member of the new work group set up to review and update the organisation's policies and practices which is headed by an external specialist.

Once all the new activities are in place, you are asked to chair a subgroup that reviews and feedback to the main group, the impact of the organisation's new practices. Having a month until the next meeting to produce a report, you set about evaluating the project's activities and identify areas for improvement or removal. In addition to producing a survey to obtain stakeholders' feedback, you also produce performance objectives for senior leaders to embed the new changes.

At the next subgroup meeting, discussions around the table indicate that other work priorities had prevented members from carrying out their reviews. So, you discuss your review proposals and apart from some minor changes, the subgroup collectively agree upon your report which is submitted to the external specialist.

A couple of months later, your manager informs you that your contribution to the organisation had been nominated for a financial recognition reward. This yearly event saw nominated employees within their peer groups recognised for their outstanding contribution to improving the services and standards of the organisation. The decision makers in this process consists of the peer group's line managers. Aware that you and a peer from another region had been nominated, you note that your peer and all the decision makers are dark skin employees but see no reason why this would affect your chances and so you wait to receive the news.

It does not take long before you learn that your peer is the winner for their valued contribution to the organisation. Your peer's accomplishment was the amalgamation of the data spreadsheets which you and your peers in other locations had populated, into one document.

Is there really any point?!! (LOL) This case serves the purpose of highlighting that the perceived less favourable treatment can occur in any general work activities.

11 – The Investigation

You provide caring support in a building where service users live independently but share communal areas. You work alongside a diverse group of people and have no great difficulty with them, although you find that some colleagues do not always carry out their duties to a high standard. On occasions you have reported incidents to your new dark skin manager but have noticed that they barely make the effort to act upon the problems, although they are a little more proactive than the former dark skin manager.

One morning whilst preparing for work, you receive a call from your manager informing you that a service user had made an accusation of theft and that it was necessary to suspend you from work whilst the matter was investigated. The incident had also been reported to the police in line with the organisation's policy and you are told that they may contact you. The name of the accuser is not disclosed to you at this time, but you are informed that an investigator will be in contact with all the relevant details.

The organisation had hired some interim workers over the recent weeks to cover the high levels of staff absences and you were aware of several incidents where service users had reported the theft of various items from their rooms. You understood the organisation's need to take precautions and protect their service users from such issues, but you are the accused on this occasion. You know that you would never do anything to cause harm or upset to any of the service users.

Two weeks after your suspension from work, a manager finally contacts you to conduct their investigation. You learn from their preliminary comments that a service user had accused you of theft and aggressive behaviour. Whilst detail of the alleged theft is disclosed, those relating to the aggressive behaviour are not, even though you ask the investigator several times about it, which makes you think the poor service user had been hospitalised. Comments about the police completing their investigation some two weeks previous is mentioned but again the investigator fails to inform you of their findings.

At the investigator's request, you provide a summary of your activities over the days leading to your suspension. You mention that the only problem you had encountered was having an increased workload when compared to your colleagues, which you felt had been unfair. You confirm having no problems with any of the service users with whom you maintained good

278

relationships. Details of colleagues, the system logs and site cameras that would confirm your whereabouts at the time of the alleged incident are provided. The investigator then asks whether you felt that you were aggressive, but when you ask them to clarify the statement, again you receive no reply.

The minutes of the investigation interview are sent for you to approve the facts discussed, but you find that they do not accurately reflect your comments. The investigator has either mis-recorded or omitted key elements of the conversation and knowing that this record will be your statement of the facts that challenges the allegation, you make the necessary corrections before returning the minutes to the investigator.

When the investigation report arrives a few days later, you are surprised to find that the statements provided by other witnesses are damning. The service user's stolen money appears to have been found by a supervisor and your line manager on the same or following day that the allegation was made, which would explain why the police never contacted you. The report also showed that only the current and former line managers had been interviewed as witnesses but none of your colleagues had been approached, which did not reflect impartiality and a balanced report. More interestingly however, is that the source of the now '*very aggressive behaviour*' allegation, did not derive from the service user who had raised the allegation of theft.

Attempting to learn more about the aggressive behaviour allegation but receiving no explanation from the investigator, had made you curious about their line of questioning. Especially as they had sought for you to reflect upon your character which implied that you had questionable behaviours which were not conducive to your line of work. Had an example of the alleged conduct been provided then you would be wiser to the facts and able to respond to the question. However, you learn from the investigation report that the formerly '*aggressive behaviour*' allegation has transformed into '*very aggressive behaviour*' and the allegation are those of your former and current line managers.

The witness statement from your former line manager alleges that you were '*very aggressive*' towards them which they claim to have raised during supervision meetings on several occasions. You do not recollect any such conversations taking place or it being documented on your meeting records, but then many colleagues had questioned the manager's competences. Likewise, your current line manager's statement that they too have spoken with you in supervision meetings about your

280

'*aggressive behaviour*', the last one taking place some months previously. Again, you recall having never had such a discussion with your line manager and you had yet to receive a copy of the report for your sign off. The investigation report findings clearly highlight a concern about your conduct which is unrelated to the service user's theft allegation. The letter accompanying the report proposes a meeting to discuss the report findings.

You ensure that you are accompanied at the meeting, ready to listen but also ready to voice your concerns about the investigation's failings. Fortunately, the newly appointed senior manager conducts the meeting and explains that lessons had been learnt from the investigation. The organisation's policy requirements meant that they must take necessary action to protect its service user, but also identified the need to protect employees. Providing you with the reassurance of being a respected and valued member of the team and employee of the organisation, the senior manager informs you that no further action would be taken with regards to the allegation.

Police involvement

Where the involvement of the police occurs because of an incident in the workplace, the organisation may withhold pertinent information from the employee whilst the police conduct their investigation. The rules and guidance relating to police involvement in workplace incidents can become complex given the role of the police services. However, where no criminal proceedings are taken, the organisation may reasonably disclose relevant information regarding the allegations to the employee.

The investigation report confirmed that the police involvement into the service user's allegation of theft was closed on the same day or the day after the allegation was made. The reason was that the alleged stolen money had been found which meant that there was no longer a case for you to answer. However, the organisation continued with their investigation into the unrelated '*very aggressive behaviour*' allegation, which did not emanate from the service user.

Investigation

The purpose of an investigation is to establish facts and to focus on the facts. It must be fair, balanced and take account of the views and actions of both the parties involved. The facts build the context which is gained from witness statements, documentary evidence of work files and records, as well as reviewing job descriptions and policies, to determine whether any misdeeds have occurred. Broadening the scope of an investigation may be necessary where the evidence collated triggers a need to delve into other areas of the employee's activities. In these instances, the employee must be informed of any additional allegations under investigation.

The report once completed, is submitted to the authorising manager who decides whether a formal process is necessary although the investigator is sometimes given this honour. Any decision must be based on the facts showing that on a balance of probability, the employee is either responsible or not, for the alleged offence. However, where there is no case to answer, but concerns about conduct are highlighted, it is not unreasonable for the manager to meet with the employee to discuss and remedy these issues.

The appointed investigator failed to follow the due process and remain impartial when establishing the facts of the service user's allegation. Knowing the theft allegation had been resolved, they continued to pursue their investigation. Rather than investigate how the allegation of '*aggressive behaviour*' found itself on the service user's complaint, the investigator conducts a fact-finding mission that centres on nothing other than the opinions of two managers. The failure to conduct interviews or to collate any other evidence in support of your statement against the claim, denied you a balanced and objective investigation which made the entire process biased and unfair.

Discrimination

The organisation has a duty not to treat one employee less favourably than another employee because of a protected characteristic. An employee must not be subjected to any detriment in the terms and conditions of their employment with the organisation. Anything done by the perpetrator of the unfair act in the course of their employment towards another employee, is treated as also being done by the organisation who will be held liable. Any claims of ignorance or the lack of understanding or incompetence in the management of an employee will not excuse or absolve the organisation of its legal responsibilities.

Pursuing a formal investigation when the case triggering the investigation is resolved, is an abuse of the delegated authority given to the investigator. Likewise, the manipulative use by the managers to weaponize the organisation's disciplinary policy to achieve a subjective outcome, is a further abuse of power which compounds the unfairness.

You had no recollection or record of any discussions held with the managers regarding the alleged aggressive behaviour concerns. Furthermore, the investigator's report presented no review meeting documents as its evidence in support of the managers' claims of your perceived behaviour. The stereotypical allegation label and the biased investigative reporting, show that on a balance of probability, the managers actions were aimed to cause you a detriment. The abuse of their delegated authority and the manipulation of the organisation's formal process show that their intentions were of a malicious nature.

As you do not share the same skin colour as the managers, then race discrimination is the reason for the treatment that you received. Whether you would have been treated differently if you shared the same skin colour is irrelevant because the less favourable treatment is evident. The abuse of the delegated authority and of the organisation's trust and values, warrants the enforcement of the zero-tolerance policy given the significant breaches to the terms and conditions of the employment contracts.

12 – Employment Tribunal

You supervise a function in a small business where temporary support is provided whenever the workload increases. You enjoy the work, and your product quality is often praised by global clients. There are two other functions led by two white skin male supervisors who each have a couple of employees in their teams that largely carry out manual work.

Following a period of absence due to a personal bereavement, you return to work and learn of the appointment of a new dark skin employee hired to work in one of the teams. On having a brief return to work discussion with your dark skin manager and owner of the business, you are informed of a clerical error and the need to adjust your forthcoming pay due to the length of your absence. Recalling that the manager had told you to take as much time as you needed, you ask whether the adjustments would take account of the company's compassionate leave entitlement. In response, your manager shouts at you which, unfortunately, begins a catalogue of problems with the manager leading to a complete breakdown in the relationship.

The problems begin with the delays in repairing the faulty equipment in your work area where you create, build, and finesse several products, most of which are used by the assembly team. The delay creates a backlog of unfinished customer products. Then false accusations of inappropriate and aggressive behaviour are levied against you when in fact you are the victim of the acts, and the perpetrators go undisciplined. A picture of a monkey is placed on the staff notice board with your name written across it alongside detrimental comments. As the dark skin perpetrator goes unpunished, their continued inappropriate behaviour creates more conflict between you and other colleagues, which your manager does nothing to rectify.

When you are told to attend an informal meeting for the actions of other staff members, you request a copy of your personnel records. The file contains malicious handwritten notes of fabricated workplace incidents for which you are blamed, which is not the personnel information you had expected to find in your file. The informal meeting turns into a formal meeting midway into discussions because you requested clarity on the nature of the misconduct you were alleged to have carried out. The manager also informs you that effective immediately, the newly appointed employee would now become your line manager. What is drawn to your attention during the process, is that your salary is significantly lower than the other two male supervisors who each supervise a couple of employees.

You raise a grievance about the mistreatment in all areas of your employment and follow the appeals process, but neither are upheld. The constant bullying behaviours of colleagues and the owner each day is such that you are left with no option but to resign your post given there is no longer any trust in the relationship.

Seeking advice from ACAS and a local citizen's advice bureau, you are provided with employment advice and assigned the support of an employment lawyer free of charge. You complete the required Employment Tribunal 1 (ET1) form clarifying that your complaint against your employer relates to: direct race discrimination, direct sex discrimination, equal pay of equal value and constructive unfair dismissal.

The first case management meeting held at the employment tribunal to discuss the case goes well. However, a couple of days before the case hearing is due to commence, you receive notification from your employment lawyer that they had decided not to represent you any further. In panic and distress, you reach out to a few contacts about your predicament and a representative offers their support.

The employment judge at the tribunal conducts a case review rather than the planned hearing given the sudden change of representatives. The judge is very understanding and offers constructive advice on the case laws and any other information you will need to evidence your claim and informs you of the new hearing date.

Prepared for the hearing, you find that you have a new dark skin employment judge presiding over your case who decides to turn the planned hearing into another case management meeting at the end of which, another hearing date is set. Whilst waiting for the hearing date to arrive, you receive communications from the tribunal about your former employer's attempt to have your claim thrown out of the tribunal on malicious grounds. Your representative counters the claim with evidence supported by case law.

Once the hearing date arrives, the day begins with the discussion of the petition from the employer which the judge denies and after checking the contents within the documents bundle, the hearing finally begins. Witnesses are called to answer questions from the employer, your representative and from the tribunal panel. The day goes well with your representative constructively challenging statements made by the witnesses and directing the panel to information contained in the bundle to counter any misleading, inaccurate, or downright lies being told by witnesses supporting the employer. Finally, skeletal arguments are read to the panel supporting each side's case before an adjournment is made so that the employment judge and panel may consider all the facts before reaching their decision.

On their return to the room, the employment judge congratulates the representatives for presenting their cases, especially your representative whom they liken to Columbo, given the *'one last thing'* style of questioning. However, whilst your representative provided a very good case, the panel rules in favour of your former employer.

The next hearing is set to deal with the equal pay issue however, the judge is not satisfied with the employer's job descriptions and decides to appoint an independent expert to produce new ones before evaluating yours and the male supervisors' jobs. Following a significant delay, a dark skin independent expert is appointed, and numerous meetings takes place to agree and challenge the duties, skills, and competences for each of the job roles.

Prior to the next hearing, you are provided with the independent expert's job evaluation report which is far from objective and devalues your role in the business. The expert has determined that your job was not rated equivalent to the male supervisors. The ratings given to the physical activity predominantly carried out in the male supervisor roles are highly scored whereas your mental agility and high educational standards are low scored, even though you had a higher requirement to create, problem solve, be analytical alongside having technical knowledge and skill.

So, you contact an organisation for assistance and sharing your concerns on reading the report, they offer the support of a specialist lawyer. However, on the day of the equal pay hearing, your dark skin lawyer fails to challenge the significant biases in the report and all the newly created information introduced into the bundle by the employer, that had not been previously disclosed to you or the tribunal panel members. As a result of this, your case for equal pay is not upheld.

By now you have no faith in this judicial process that is supposed to protect vulnerable people from unscrupulous employers and believe that continuing this process would serve only to provide you with another injustice. You have also learnt from overhearing the chatter amongst tribunal staff in the coffee shop next door, that your former boss and the judge presiding in your case are firm associates who like to share secret handshakes under the table. So, on the eve of the final hearing to deal with your constructive dismissal claim, you decide to withdraw from the process. Whilst you believed that the claim would be won in your favour, the lack of trust and the perceived bias decisions making meant that you no longer had any confidence in the outcome. For the sake of your own sanity, you decide to get on with life.

Employment Tribunal

Employment Tribunals are the venue where employees enter when they are dissatisfied with the outcome of the organisation's formal disciplinary or grievance processes and perceived breaches of the employment contract. They are a means of seeking independent and impartial resolution to a complaint of unfair treatment in the workplace.

The tribunal panel usually consists of a chairperson now called an employment judge who is a specialist in employment law. The judge is the person who decides whether a complaint is a matter of discrimination. They may be accompanied by panel members who are a trade union specialist and or an employer of a business. Tribunals are expected to deal with cases impartially and justly using their expertise and knowledge of the law to resolve disputes.

Tribunals provide for employees and the organisations whom the claim is against, to represent themselves throughout the process and are provided with guidance on any actions necessary prior to a hearing. However, the formalities adopted in tribunals with the alien law language and procedures not familiar to the common person, makes this process less of a discussion around a large table as intended, and more of a courtroom drama series. It is for this reason that legal representatives acting on behalf of the disputing parties frequent the tribunal setting.

With regards to your claim, the tribunal members failed to fully consider the facts of your complaint, the context of incidents at the time that they occurred and their impact on you. Instead, it accepted the employer's newly created policy documents and other material that influenced the perception of credibility whilst distorting the facts of the matter. Irrespective of your representative's successful challenges to this illusion, the tribunal ruled in favour of the former employer which made their decisions unfair.

293

Independent Expert

The independent experts are specialist who conducts job evaluations to determine equal pay claims. Equal pay issues may relate to pay, the value and the rating of the role and is typically used to compare the pay between women and men. The imperative is that the evaluation must be bias free and based on fair and sound judgement. The job evaluation does not consider the sex of the person performing the job, but those competences required to carry out the job such as responsibilities, decision making, knowledge and skills which are scored against factors such as expertise, decision, autonomy, responsibility, and interpersonal skills.

The job evaluation report assessing yours and the male comparators' supervisory roles, determined that your role was not of equal value. The expert's analysis of the roles was cemented in biased traditions of male physicality and the perceived incapabilities of women. The report should have been rejected by the tribunal panel on the grounds that it was unreliable, which is why the ruling in favour of the former employer was unfair.

Complaint Handling General Guidance

Every person desire to be treated with civility and fairness in everyday life and in any given situation, whether accessing a service or when working for an organisation. The unfortunate reality is that such desires are not always a given. Raising a complaint provides the opportunity for concerns about any mistreatment received to be heard, and for explanations and compensation if appropriate, to be offered as a resolution.

In many workplace settings, employees will avoid making a complaint because they have learnt to accept the difference in the treatment they receive. Accepting this behaviour allows those responsible for the mistreatment to continue applying it to other employees, which then becomes a normal behavioural practice in the workplace unless it is stopped. Emancipate yourselves and others from such treatment.

These case experiences are lessons to learn from so that if you find yourself in a similar situation, you will have a better understanding of how to identify and overcome the barriers to achieve a fair outcome. Where you are treated less favourably in the workplace, here are some practical steps towards reaching solutions. The important thing to do is to act.

1. **Speak**: If an action or behaviour by an employee of the organisation upsets you in a particular way, have a polite conversation with the employee to let them know how their comments or actions upset you. It is not unusual for misunderstandings to occur in the workplace, and it is likely that the matter will be easily resolved. Ignoring upsetting comments or behaviours just to maintain cordial relationships with others may seem sensible but this gives permission to the perpetrators to continue with the unwanted behaviour if left unchallenged. Likewise, if you observe the mistreatment of others taking place, then act and speak out.

2. **Keep a Record:** Where the problem is of a more serious nature or the unwanted conduct persists, then make sure that you keep a record of each incident. The date, details of each incident, the people who witnessed the incident are important including notes of any comments made at the time and or any supporting documents such as emails and reports. These will help to build your evidence for the complaint.

3. **Support:** Speak to someone that is trustworthy and impartial. Sometimes you can second guess yourself either because you may think that the act towards you was a figment of your imagination, or you may think that no one will believe your side

of the story. Either way, speak to someone whom you trust and who can provide you with constructive advice, be they friends, relatives, or a mentor. Speaking to someone provides you with a sounding board to debate and analyse your concerns in addition to easing your stress level. Having a conversation with organisations such as the Citizens Advice Bureaux, ACAS or the Equality and Human Rights Commission is always useful for general information and guidance. Access to the occupational health service provided to all employees by the organisation, is an additional support for managing your mental and general wellbeing, where counselling and financial guidance may also be accessed.

4. **Company Policies**: Policies and procedures are the rules of the organisation that apply to all employees. The grievance or the dignity at work policies are those which are used for raising a complaint about unwanted or unfair conduct by fellow employees, irrespective of the level at which they operate in the organisation. Ensure that you retain a copy of the policy so that you have a clear understanding of the steps that you will need to take when raising a complaint and how it will be handled by the organisation. These procedures are based on a process of fairness and natural justice, where both parties put forward and defend a

complaint. The complaint handling process aligns to the recommended best practices advocated by ACAS whose website provides the guidance in more detail. Should the organisation fail to follow this process, for whatever reason, then any claim for damages, should it be successful at an employment tribunal, will be increased by a decent percentage.

5. **Other Policies & Documents**: It will be useful to obtain copies of other organisational policy documents in support of your complaint, depending on the nature of the unwanted or unfair treatment. The organisation's values, senior manager's code of conduct, equality, diversity, and inclusion commitments are all useful policies or strategies that the organisation expects its employees to follow. If your complaint identifies failures in these or other areas, then the policies will be of assistance.

6. **Representation**: Trade unions or employee representatives in organisations can be a great source of assistance in providing guidance and practical support. Discussions with representatives at the initial stages of any workplace problem may, with your consent, result in an informal discussion with a manager or the employee to resolve the problem. This obviously will be dependent upon the act or behaviour in question. If you find your representative unhelpful or inactive in providing you

with meaningful support, then contact your local trade union office. You should express your concerns and to seek an alternative representative to support you with your case. Paying a union subscription entitles you to many benefits but the primary one is that of constructive and meaningful support when dealing with a workplace problem.

7. **Investigation**: The investigation meeting provides you with the opportunity to present all the information you have collected regarding your experience of the unfair treatment and to explain how its impact has affected you with regards to your performance, wellbeing etc. You will be provided with a copy of the notes taken in the meeting. It is important to be aware that whilst the meeting notes will not be a record of each spoken word, it will summarise the main points discussed. If you believe that key points have been missed or not recorded properly to reflect the conversation, you can amend the record to reflect your views accurately before it is returned to the investigator.

8. **Hearings**: Following the investigation where the decision is reached to hold a hearing, a copy of the investigation report should be provided to you together with the evidence collected. You have the right to be accompanied at the hearing usually by a recognised union representative or a work colleague. Where

299

the employer provides a reasonable explanation for the unfair treatment and proposes to make further improvements, you may be satisfied with the outcome and decide to take no further action. Where you remain dissatisfied with the outcome, you have the right to appeal against the decision. The reason for the appeal must be based on either the law or information provided but not considered by the hearing panel.

9. **Employment Tribunal**: If the appeal decision is still not to your satisfaction, you may decide to take your case to an employment tribunal for consideration. The claim to an employment tribunal must be based on the evidence of an injustice that breach your employment contract e.g., discrimination, unfair dismissal, equal pay, redundancy. Please know that if you make a claim that is false or malicious about your employer, the tribunal may issue a heavy financial penalty against you. The tribunal process commences with the completion of an ET1 form detailing your claim (the claimant) against your employing organisation (the respondent). You will have three months from the last act of the unfair treatment or of the ending of your employment contract to submit the form. The sooner the form is completed, which some employees are known to act upon when raising their grievance appeal, the better.

300

DO YOU GET IT?

Completion of the ET1 will also trigger the involvement of ACAS.

10. **The Advisory, Conciliation and Arbitration Service (ACAS)** provide services of mediation and giving advice and information on employment issues. On receipt of the ET1, ACAS will provide you with a certificate and processes will commence to attempt to settle the dispute between you and the organisation before it progresses to a tribunal hearing.

11. **Settlement**: A financial settlement known as a settlement agreement may be offered to you by the organisation to avoid a tribunal hearing. This is not necessarily an admittance of guilt, but an avoidance of the financial cost placed on the organisation associated with hiring a lawyer or legal team to defend the claim. The financial cost to the organisation for the business days lost for the hearing, the employees who must attend the hearing as witnesses etc will also factor in the settlement decision. Likewise, if you choose to self- represent your claim, or have a legal representative act on your behalf, an equal amount of time, attention and costs will be necessary for the preparation of the hearing.

12. **Be Proactive:** Whether you decide to continue with your employment tribunal claim or not, it is important to note that

from the moment you complete the ET1 form, you must deal with and respond to all communications from the employment tribunal, ACAS and any legal representatives involved with the claim, promptly. A failure to respond to communications promptly and without just cause may result in the employment tribunal throwing out your claim. Complacency wins you nothing.

13 **Do the Right Thing**: Never forget the reason you are pursuing a case through an employment tribunal, which is because of an injustice caused to you and to prevent it from happening to anyone else. You may be one person against an employing organisation, but you a giant in the fight for equality, fairness, and inclusion, which is nothing but admirable. Remember, you are never alone in this cause.

CHAPTER 14

Now, Do You Get It?

This has been a strange journey of introspection for me because the more I thought about the challenges endured in my work life the more they reflected my childhood experiences of racism. The childish games were the same, only the environment had altered.

My efforts to develop, progress and achieve within organisations just like any other employee on the workplace level playing field, was denied. This privilege was afforded only to a preferred group of employees, and it did not matter that I was just as competent or more experienced or had the same or higher qualification. There was an expectation of subservience and acceptance of manipulated organisational rules.

Challenging any less favourable treatment meant being subjected to offensive behaviours and further detriment that no employee should have to endure, never mind one with a protected characteristic. No level playing field existed because the evidence that countered the preconditioned biases towards my skin colour could not be accepted by those in positions of influence. Those employees tasked with the organisation's public commitment towards equality, diversity, and inclusion.

303

The reason for their conduct, whether out of hate, envy, or just being devoid of any human consciousness, were persistent. Being the only source of difference within a department made me an easy target as other black employees tended to be either temporary workers or segmented in low paying jobs if they were not carrying out domestic work. Whether working as an employee or a contractor, this was the depressive picture of black employment. Whilst some changes have occurred as I watch my younger family members enter managerial positions, they too are being plagued by the uneven playing field antics. It is no wonder that the younger generation seek independent career paths which are deemed preferable to an unbalanced and biased commitment to an organisation.

My experiences of racism in the workplace, and the public reports of disproportionate treatment within organisations, proves that there is still much work to be done to eliminate racism and the other discriminatory conduct within organisations. Creating an external illusion with published one-off gestures, meaningless statements, or the occasional picture of a dark skin person on websites to reflect the inclusion of difference, does not demonstrate a credible commitment when the internal culture and traditions of treating difference negatively remains embedded within the organisation.

Whenever I read a book that explains a subject matter, I like to know exactly what action is needed to resolve a problem. It would be remiss of me, therefore if I did not provide some guidance on resolving discrimination in the workplace, although much has already been provided throughout this book. So, to summarise.

1. Be mindful that the organisational culture reflects one of inclusion and not exclusion. The morals and the standards that senior executives conveyed to the entire workforce is important in setting the tone to all. Conveying the aspiration of winning at all costs, instils a Machiavellian attitude where competitiveness is seen as the elimination of all perceived threats to achieve a perceived status. This achieves nothing more than a toxic environment where no employee is safe. An inclusive environment where there is an effective collaboration of diverse talents that achieves the organisation's objectives would be a more welcoming and successful change.

2. Accountability and responsibility for equality and inclusion must be firmly placed on the organisation's agenda. Managers must be held to account for any failing standards where targets

are not achieved. If you require a benchmark to work towards, then using regional rather than national population statistics to build a representative workforce would a reasonable starting place. Complacency has no role in building an inclusive workforce unlike zero tolerance who should be firmly seated at the high table.

3. Development in equality and inclusion of the workforce is imperative as not all employees will have engaged with diverse cultures and may retain a bias towards difference. Establishing a foundation of inclusion awareness training from the outset of employment combined with an emphasis of zero tolerance towards racism and any other discriminatory conduct will move the organisation in the right direction. It is also important that employees are not showcased because of their difference. On entering employment, these employees are and should be treated no differently to the rest of the workforce, hence the level playing field. With the exception of course, of those employees who require reasonable adjustments. Their talent got them through the doors of the organisation so allow their talent to flourish and not be diminished with tokenism.

4. Management is the cornerstone of an effective team and as with the achievement of operational targets or projects, they

must be held to account for any discrimination in their department or team. Auditing recruitment, probation and performance appraisal reviews, development, formal action and exit interviews of team and departmental members is essential to determine whether bias rather than fairness has influenced decisions pertaining to diverse employees. Zero tolerance.

5. Human Resources is responsible for upholding the moral and ethical standards of fairness of all workforce members thereby upholding the organisation's values towards inclusion. Leaders within this department must have a sound understanding of employment laws to ensure practices and behaviours adopted by the organisation's members are not abused or mismanaged but are equitably balanced for all workforce members.

6. Recruitment is the first barrier to accessing employment which must be reviewed to ensure the acceptance of difference. Where this function is outsourced, ensure candidates are not restricted or caused a detriment because of any additional requirements imposed by recruitment organisations acting on the organisation's behalf. The integrity of the recruitment standards that would usually be in place with an inhouse service should not be compromised.

7. Pay must be reviewed to ensure that it is fair and equitably applied to all employees. The lowest pay scale must start with a salary equivalent to a living wage, irrespective of the type of job whether apprentice or cleaner.

Now, do you get it? It is not so difficult to understand. Treat all people in the same manner that you expect to be treated. With dignity and respect.

This book aimed to enlighten its readers of my personal experience of racism in the workplace so that a better understanding of this toxic attitude can be achieved and be effectively eliminated from structures, once and for all. Taking such steps will achieve inclusion where all employees may fulfil personal and corporate ambitions without suffering a detriment.

As I write these last few lines, the beautiful voice of Dennis Brown is singing, *'No man is an island'* on my radio, which is so true. Every successful business began from the creation of an idea. The idea became bigger when other people's opinions were explored before it became a reality. This reality could only be achieved with the engagement of other specialists and the more growth it achieved the more people appointed to support the progression of the idea. It is the support, the knowledge the skills and commitment of other people, the workforce, operating

308

together that maintains the success, and the financial wealth of the idea.

The ideas, that is organisations in their traditional forms and in all sectors, are beginning to crumble now that illusions are being shattered and immoral behaviours are exposed. Skilled workers' exodus, and disruptive strike actions are just some of the protestations against authoritarian and toxic rule, which will continue unless meaningful change occurs to balance the scales. Now is the time to destroy all the outdated systems of illusion so that equality for all people is truly valued and respected.

I truly hope that you now get it and will eliminate the problem of racism and any other form of discrimination within the workplace, because I am done with it. I am destined for a new career path where the toxicity of the past will form no part of my future. I hope you can do likewise within the workplace.

'

References

Books

Dabiri, E. (2021) *What White People Can Do Next from Allyship to Coalition* London, Bloomsbury Publishing

Kidner, R (2021) *Blackstone Statutes on Employment Law 2021-2022* 31st Ed. Oxford, Oxford University Press

Lockton, D.J. (2014) *Employment Law* 9th Ed. Basingstoke, Palgrave Macmillan

Rothenberg, P. S, (2016) White Privilege 5th Ed. New York, Worth Publishers

Liff, S, (1996) 'Two routes to managing diversity: individual differences or social group characteristics', Warwick University

Website Articles

Pfizer accused of pandemic profiteering as profits double | Pfizer | The Guardian https://www.theguardian.com/business/2022/feb/08/

Windrush generation: Who are they and why are they facing problems? - BBC News https: www.bbc.co.uk - 4378221

NHS risks losing one third of ethnic minority doctors due to racism, finds BMA report - BMA media centre - BMA https: www bma.org.uk/bma-media-centre/

'Race inequalities and ethnic disparities in healthcare - Race equality in medicine - BMA https: www bma.org.uk/bma-media-centre/

Ethnic inequalities in health in later life, 1993–2017: the persistence of health disadvantage over more than two decades | Ageing & Society | http:www.cambridge.core/journals/ageing-and-society/

NHS risks losing one third of ethnic minority doctors due to racism, finds BMA report https: www bma.org.uk/bma-media-centre/

Nationality and Borders Bill: equality impact assessment - GOV.UK https://www.gov.uk/government/publications/

West must force private lenders to ease Africa's crippling debt, say campaigners | Global development | The Guardian. https://www.theguardian.com/global-development/2022/jul/12/

Qatar World Cup Chief Publicly Admits High Migrant Death Tolls | Human Rights Watch (hrw.org) https://www.hrw.org/news/2022/11/30/

African governments owe three times more debt to private
lenders   than   China   -   Debt   Justice/   .
https://debtjustice.org.uk/press-release/

https://www.cipd.co.uk/

https://www.acas.org.uk/

https://www.equalityhumanrights.com/en

Films & Documentaries

An Inspector Calls (1954), David Lean, Shepperton
Studios, British Lions Films

Hobson's Choice (1954) Guy Hamilton, Shepperton
Studios, British Lions Films

'*Unremembered - Britain's Forgotten War Heroes*'| All 4
(channel4.com)

DO YOU GET IT?

About the Author

Born in Birmingham, England to Jamaican parents, Barbara McDonald was a Business Studies & Finance student at Handsworth Technical College. On relocating to the North of England, Barbara acquired a Batchelor's degree in Business Studies & Finance with Human Resource Management before obtaining a Master degree in, Human Resource Management from Manchester Metropolitan University. As an Associate member of the Chartered Institute of Personnel and Development, Barbara has spent the past 18 years working in various HR and Equality roles in the UK.

Printed in Great Britain
by Amazon

26438341R00183